JAMES WHEELER

LORDSHIP MATTERS

HIS NAME. HIS NATURE. OUR NEED.

Lordship Matters
His Name. His Nature. Our Need.

Copyright © 2020 by James Wheeler

Published by Clay Bridges in Houston, TX
www.ClayBridgesPress.com

All rights reserved. No part of this publication may be reproduced, stored in a retrieval system, or transmitted in any form by any means, electronic, mechanical, photocopy, recording, or otherwise, without the prior permission of the publisher, except as provided for by USA copyright law.

ISBN: 978-1-939815-93-4
eISBN: 978-1-939815-87-3

Unless otherwise indicated, all Scripture quotations are taken from the Holy Bible, New International Version®, NIV®. Copyright © 1973, 1978, 1984, 2011 by Biblica, Inc.™ Used by permission of Zondervan. All rights reserved worldwide. www.zondervan.com The "NIV" and "New International Version" are trademarks registered in the United States Patent and Trademark Office by Biblica, Inc.™

Scripture quotations marked (AMP) are taken from the Amplified® Bible (AMP), Copyright © 2015 by The Lockman Foundation. Used by permission. www.Lockman.org

Scripture quotations marked (AMPC) are taken from the Amplified® Bible (AMPC), Copyright © 1954, 1958, 1962, 1964, 1965, 1987 by The Lockman Foundation. Used by permission. www.Lockman.org

Scripture quotations marked (CSB) are taken from the Christian Standard Bible®, Copyright © 2017 by Holman Bible Publishers. Used by permission. Christian Standard Bible® and CSB® are federally registered trademarks of Holman Bible Publishers.

Scripture quotations marked (ESV) are taken from the ESV® Bible (The Holy Bible, English Standard Version®), copyright © 2001 by Crossway, a publishing ministry of Good News Publishers. Used by permission. All rights reserved.

Scripture quotations marked (KJV) are taken from the King James Version (KJV): King James Version, public domain.

Scripture quotations marked (NASB) are taken from the New American Standard Bible® (NASB), Copyright © 1960, 1962, 1963, 1968, 1971, 1972, 1973, 1975, 1977, 1995 by The Lockman Foundation. Used by permission. www.Lockman.org.

Scripture quotations marked (NKJV) are taken from the New King James Version®. Copyright © 1982 by Thomas Nelson. Used by permission. All rights reserved.

Scripture quotations marked (NLT) are taken from the Holy Bible, New Living Translation, copyright ©1996, 2004, 2007, 2013, 2015 by Tyndale House Foundation. Used by permission of Tyndale House Publishers, Inc., Carol Stream, Illinois 60188. All rights reserved.

Special Sales: Most Clay Bridges titles are available in special quantity discounts. Custom imprinting or excerpting can also be done to fit special needs. Contact Clay Bridges at Info@ClayBridgesPress.com.

This book is dedicated in loving memory to my dad, Roger B. Wheeler. Dad, when you made Jesus Christ the Lord of your life, the world changed. Your life, like George Bailey's, was not only wonderful in its earthly brevity but is eternally wonderful because of Jesus. And so is ours. Your legacy lives on through this book. The lives that are changed because of it will be eternal fruit for the kingdom of heaven.

Table of Contents

Introduction		1
Chapter One	Essential Elements	7
Chapter Two	The Law of Lordship Overview	17
Chapter Three	The Name of the Lord Is the Nature of the Lord	25
Chapter Four	Our Need: The Nature of the Lord Is Our Need for the Lord	39
Chapter Five	Releasing Salvation: The Need for the Lord in Us Is the Need of the Lord through Us	53
Chapter Six	Wisdom: The Lord of Wisdom	73
Chapter Seven	Finally	85
Acknowledgments		91

Introduction

At the tender age of six, on the front steps of my family's modest rental, I asked Jesus into my heart and invited Him to be my Lord and Savior. I didn't know it at the time, but later I would struggle with understanding just what was supposed to have taken place that day.

As a young man growing up in the Midwest, I was curious about what new experiences the world might have in store beyond the confines of the tiny, blue-collar agricultural town of Clinton, Iowa, on the banks of the Mississippi River. Not that I was a mistrusting person, but I often had a sense that the Christian faith might contain something more personally meaningful to me than what I had experienced in my small-town, Pentecostal church in the early '70s.

During adolescence and into my young-adult years, I eventually learned that my curiosity about the world and even those apparent trust issues were not bad things to be wrestling with. Actually, they displayed a healthy and vital part of God's unique wiring in me. God made me to be a discoverer, a discerner, a deep thinker, and a seeker of solutions. Through my eyes, perplexities presented themselves as puzzles just crying out for me to solve them.

In the years following my confession of faith as a little boy, I often wondered if it had been real. Was I truly "saved"? I had come to believe God was real, but everything else about how I should live out my faith left me with more questions than satisfying answers.

As a teenager, I rebelled against the kind of lifestyle prohibitions that came with the teachings of evangelical Christianity. I wanted to drink deeply of the world and live a passionate existence that felt more fulfilling than the life of the good Sunday school boy I once was.

I continued the cycle of secret rebellion on and off for many years. Each cycle ended with guilt, shame, and often severe consequences for my actions. Feeling convicted of doing wrong, I would come to repentance on some level, only to be left with no compelling sense of life's purpose.

As I reflect today, I suppose the heart of my question was this: I am saved from sin and death, but what exactly am I saved to? My impression was that my future held gold streets and sitting on fluffy clouds, which did not excite me. Escaping eternity in hell was a comfort, for sure. But I needed to have a greater purpose for my life besides recruiting people to join what I viewed as a not-so-engaging insiders' club. Much has changed since then.

At the writing of this introduction, it is now the summer of 2019. I am a man in my 50s raising a vibrant, creative, nine-year-old daughter with my wife of 26 years. I have been in full-time ministry most of my married life. I'm here to tell you how grateful I am for the answers I found as a result of my sincere pursuit of God—a God whom I have come to know as very real, loving, patient, and purposeful, a God who does have deep and meaningful answers, a God who has made available the source of life to everyone who asks.

Through it all, I have determined that this life source comes not from the constructs and rituals of religion but from a potentially deep and purposeful relationship offered through salvation in Jesus Christ.

Do I have the perfect answer for every question? Absolutely not. But a few years back, I believe the Lord ministered to me some powerful truths about lordship and salvation. I saw truths from His Word that came to light in such a profoundly impactful way that I knew I had to write a book about them.

Because of these powerful truths, a lifetime of puzzling questions are being answered. My prayer life has become richer and more vibrant. My roles as leader in my family, covenant partner with my wife, father of my child, and pastor in the church have all grown healthier and more effective.

Introduction

The inspiration for this book began on a series of commutes I made to attend a weekend conference near my hometown. The trip was short enough to drive and more economical than booking a hotel room for one night. The round trip was about two-and-a-half hours, and I made the trip up and back on a Friday night and then again the next day.

For some reason, I couldn't keep music on in the car. As a worship leader, I'm often involved in listening to and preparing music for worship. Yet as an introvert, I often opt for silence over music on long car rides. That was the case on this particular trip. But more than that, it seemed that in the quiet, the Lord was speaking to my heart. He was asking me to inquire of Him.

In the back of my mind, I recalled what the Lord had spoken to me a month before at the end of April when I awoke early one morning. He quietly spoke in my spirit, "I am about to bless your socks off." It was subtle yet matter-of-fact. With my spiritual ears, I clearly heard Him repeat that exact phrase three or four times.

Remembering that phrase, I intentionally quieted my heart and decided to pray. I began thanking God for telling me what He was going to do. I had been in the Christian faith long enough to have made just about every mistake possible when it comes to hearing from God and finding His will for my life. I've chased dreams that were mine, not His. I have blown tests in faithfulness over and over again. Too often, I have let my personality push ahead instead of resting in the timing of the Lord. Those painful life experiences have encouraged me to take precautions, slow down, and tune my ears patiently to the voice of wisdom.

As I began to pray in my car that day, I thought of Solomon, who could have asked for anything, and the Lord would have granted it. But Solomon asked for wisdom. And so, for a period of time, I began to call out for wisdom. The method I chose felt ridiculous. I started yelling in the car, "Wisdom, I need you! Insight, where are you? Understanding, come to me! Make yourself known!"

As I called out and continued to pray during those commutes, a new understanding began to unfold for me. My mind was being renewed to some vital truths in God's Word. I was getting a fresh insight into familiar scripture passages I knew were there but had not realized they held greater significance.

He was amplifying and bringing my focus to an area that would establish a new level of maturity in my walk with Him. He certainly was blessing my socks off! It all started with simple obedience to His Word as I called on Him. Look what this passage from Proverbs says: "Indeed, if you call out for insight and cry aloud for understanding" (Prov. 2:3).

So I called out. Suddenly, the familiar salvation passages were coming alive in a deeper way. I started to see clearly that this moment of calling on the Lord followed by His overwhelming response to me was lordship and salvation in action. My mind was being saved, or made whole, to the Law of Lordship. As I called upon the Lord, upon my Lord Jesus as wisdom, I was being saved—not for the first time but in a way that released a new dimension of kingdom wholeness in me. My heart was repentant of my own sinful, lacking ways, and I became desperate for Him to be wisdom as the source of my true need. "Everyone who calls on the name of the Lord will be saved" (Rom. 10:13).

What started out as calling aloud for wisdom and insight eventually led to the major premise of this book. Among other names I called out in the car that day was the simple cry for help. I cried aloud for help repeatedly.

I have a vibrant little girl who often calls me from another part of the house. I know she needs me when she calls because she is mine. She can say "Daddy!" or she can just say "I need help in here!" In fact, if she just sighs in a certain way, I hear her. And when I hear her call, I can't wait to respond to her need. She needs me, and she calls on me out of the belief in our established relationship—a healthy, strong, and ever-growing intimate relationship.

Just like I respond to my daughter's cries for me, the Lord answered my cries. Help was coming to me in the car that day because I cried to the name of the Lord Jesus, my helper. "My help comes from the LORD, the Maker of heaven and earth" (Ps. 121:2).

Maybe your life as a Christian has fallen flat. Or maybe, like me, you are wired to pursue answers beyond what is commonly accepted. Perhaps you have struggles and patterns in your life that don't make sense or challenges that feel impossible to break through. Do you sense a nagging inside when questions aren't reconciled in a deeper, more complete way?

Introduction

If that is you, I want to share three simple yet deep and powerful truths about salvation that I believe will positively stretch your understanding. They will help you trace the source of those struggles and empower you to walk in a fuller expression of salvation in Christ Jesus than ever before.

May the contents of this book serve as a kind of falling-into-place, very satisfying piece of the puzzle. I pray it will strengthen and encourage your faith journey as a confessor of Jesus Christ, a follower of Him as Lord, and as one who experiences the fullness of the kind of salvation He has to offer.

CHAPTER ONE

Essential Elements

If you declare with your mouth, "Jesus is Lord," and believe in your heart that God raised him from the dead, you will be saved. For it is with your heart that you believe and are justified, and it is with your mouth that you profess your faith and are saved.
—Rom. 10:9–10

Everyone who calls on the name of the Lord will be saved.
—Rom. 10:13

These verses contain what many believers recognize as the most significant passages in all of scripture that pertain to salvation. To build a foundation for what the Lord showed me about the three matters that make up the Law of Lordship, it's helpful to understand the universal truths they speak of.

These concepts can be written as the following statements that continuously affirm, identify, and reinforce one another:

- Whoever is confessed (called upon) as lord will be the one saving.
- Whatever the heart hears (is exposed to), the heart will believe (live by).
- Whatever the heart believes, the mouth will say.
- Whatever the mouth says, the heart will believe.
- Whoever is recognized as the savior, the heart will need.
- Whoever the heart needs, it will call upon.

Together, these concepts help diagnose the results of the contents of our words, the belief system of our hearts, and the source of life we identify as Savior and Lord. They reveal our manner of living. Every second of our lives can be diagrammed with these concepts—concepts that God established from the beginning of time in order to ordain and order life according to His Word. It is from these concepts that the three simple matters that make up the Law of Lordship emerge. But first, let's look more closely at lordship.

Lord as Authority

Many cultures throughout history have defined the title *lord* as an appellation for a person or deity who has authority, control, or power over others, acting like a master, a chief, or a ruler. The appellation can also denote certain persons who hold a title of the peerage in the United Kingdom or who are entitled to courtesy titles. The collective term *lords* can refer to a group or body of peers.

In simplest terms, lordship is a form of authority. Lordship is about the established ruler (lord) as well as the kingdom (salvation, wholeness) created by such a rule. The one who is defined or declared as lord determines empowerment and potential release of authority. And whoever is defined and declared as lord will establish the kingdom and type of living conditions for those who live under that rule of lordship.

Lordship is both a command and a self-reinforcing truth. Whoever we have confessed as lord will be the object of our complete affection and love. We will sacrifice our time, give our attention, and offer the best of who we are to whoever is lord. That truth is evident in the drug addict, the sex addict, and the social media addict. It is manifest in the insecure control freak at the office and the narcissist. It is apparent in the workaholic and the needy congregant who loves to offer prayer requests more than see them answered.

What is worshipped, honored, and given space, place, time, attention, latitude, and influence will create a habitation or kingdom. And kingdom habitation empowers the laws of the kingdom or government that we have agreed to live by.

Lords come when we call because we live in a place where we have created a dependence on them and have developed a relationship with them based on our beliefs and our confessions. The fact that we call on them releases them into a leading influence in our lives.

Lordship works in a self-defining, self-reinforcing set of principles. Lordship both establishes relationships and reinforces and grows existing relationships. This principle is highlighted by the following truth about faith: "So then faith comes by hearing, and hearing by the word of God" (Rom. 10:17 NKJV).

This is key: We will be saved by whom we call upon. But we will be kept by whom we keep calling upon. "To him who is able to keep you" (Jude 1:24).

The Lord is able to keep us if we are willing to keep calling on Him. The Lord who saves us is the One we believe in and continually call upon. It might be easier to see it paraphrased without the specific context of God's Word, something like this: "The way we live, the driving conviction of our lives, is the result of what we believe to be truth."

Our belief system is enforced by our obedience to that system. And our mouths call out what our heart-beliefs are firmly locked into. "It is written: 'I believed; therefore I have spoken.' Since we have that same spirit of faith, we also believe and therefore speak" (2 Cor. 4:13).

Belief

There is an old, Middle-English word that can help us understand how beliefs are what we live by. The word is *bileave*, which means to "be-leave" or "live-by." Knowing the root word helps simplify our understanding of how belief systems are developed, nourished, fed, and grown.

We live by what we believe, and we will come to believe what we live by. If our lives are near to the influences of the world, our hearts will be living in the world or believing in the world.

Remember, we are in this world but not of this world (John 17:16). If we spend more time exposed to, exalting, magnifying, and developing intimacy with God and His kingdom, we will operate and flow in the full benefits of His kingdom and under the blessing of His lordship.

The source of our belief bears witness with the Spirit who birthed that belief. Our inner witness will align with the author and releaser of the belief we partner ourselves with. "The Spirit himself bears witness with our spirit that we are children of God" (Rom. 8:16 ESV).

Another way to look at it is that we partner with the power that offers life to us. We do that by speaking out and calling on what our heart has the most revelation of at that time. This witness-bearing and calling points directly to whomever—or whatever—lord you have called upon.

The god (lord) of this age, Satan, has been given power (2 Cor. 4:4, Eph. 2:2). At his disposal are a host of potentially named lords who will respond to our confessed heart-beliefs. Yet Jesus has been given the name that is above all other names.

The Position of Jesus Christ as Lord

This statement—Jesus Christ is Lord to the glory of God the Father—is an eternal truth. His Lordship is undisputed, unquestionable, and undeniable.

> *Therefore, God elevated him [Jesus] to the place of highest honor and gave him the name above all other names, that at the name of Jesus every knee should bow, in heaven and on earth and under the earth, and every tongue declare that Jesus Christ is Lord, to the glory of God the Father.*
>
> —Phil. 2:9–11 NLT

A lord who goes unsurrendered to is lord in position and title only. A lord whose kingdom hasn't been fully entered into will have limited influence. Likewise, an attempt at serving multiple lords and living in multiple competing kingdoms is a recipe for self-destruction.

The purpose of God elevating Jesus and giving preeminence to His name was not just to make His standing as Lord known. It also was so all creation would awaken to the truth and be empowered to release His rule in our personal lives as well as in every sphere of influence we have been given.

Presently, the lordship of Jesus Christ isn't forced on all humanity—it is chosen by comparatively few. One day in eternity, however, everyone will confess that Jesus Christ is Lord. For now, the fullness of this experience is entirely up to the believer and confessor of this truth.

There is a short window of time for us to willingly confess His lordship and experience salvation on earth as it already is eternally in heaven. God allowed us this opportunity so His kingdom would expand redemptively (in cooperation with His redemptive purpose) through us in the Church Age.

When the Church Age is complete, Christ will return and forcibly take back the fullness of His kingdom from those who remain in opposition.

If, in the end, the kingdom didn't expand or multiply as a result of releasing the gift of salvation, then salvation's confession would have remained somewhat limited. In other words, some will have greatly multiplied the gift of salvation that was given to them by consistently and faithfully expanding the kingdom of God, and others will have neglected those possibilities entirely.

Revealed Truth Reveals the True Lord

Why is this? Because truth must be revealed, not merely released. A revealed truth has the potential to become a lived truth. On the other hand, a released truth is merely the passing on of information; it is merely communication, devoid of transformation.

> *Simon Peter answered, "You are the Messiah, the Son of the living God." Jesus replied, "You are blessed . . . because my Father in heaven has revealed this to you."*
>
> —Matt. 16:16–17 NLT

Simon Peter was gloriously and authentically transformed after a powerful encounter that led to repentance followed by a complete surrender of his life. No sinner's prayer in the way we have come to know it was required. Peter just released a confessed heart-revelation. He came to the sudden realization that everything Jesus was, was everything he needed.

Peter's declaration was the summary of the reality he had come to know and believe. The statement didn't make it so; it simply affirmed that the truth was, indeed, so.

Before this revelation, Peter was surely confessing certain ideas, believing in something and following the lords released by his understanding. He was walking in salvation, or wholeness, to his current confessed heart-belief, but not yet to the revelation of Jesus Christ as Lord.

Maybe one of the lords in Peter's life was the identity he valued from his legacy as an expert fisherman. Perhaps his perception of the world around him was the kingdom he was saved to. The system of the world and the religious traditions of the day made up the beliefs that centered his life in a complete and whole way.

But in that shining moment, everything Peter knew, everything he thought he believed suddenly shifted. And from the depths of his heart, he proclaimed the truest statement that anyone could utter, perhaps something like this: "Yes, You, Jesus Christ, are Lord!"

Have you ever had an aha moment? A revelation? Sometimes, my daughter says, "Oh, I get it now!" As she grows, she has more context for the things she is being exposed to in movies. Jokes that went over her head when she was three make her laugh now. She can make a connection between the sense that this should be funny and the reality of "Wow! This is really funny, and I get it!"

I had my own aha moment recently when I decided to make some severe dietary changes—changes no one would have ever predicted from a guy whose idea of heaven involved bacon and donuts. I had a nagging sense that even though I wasn't overweight, I was extremely unhealthy on the inside. My diet, age, and family history all spoke of a potential health crisis in the future that I desperately wanted to avoid. So, I began searching for a truth related to my health journey.

It wasn't until I found a functional, integrative doctor and went through hours of consulting and testing that it hit me. This was for real, and I needed to make immediate and permanent changes. This revelation was so compelling that I immediately made the drastic changes required.

Before that time, I could tell you all about healthy choices and mimic others in conversations regarding health. But the truth I knew wasn't alive enough in me to make a change. That is the difference between releasing truth and what takes place when someone is awakened to a revealed truth.

Recited words devoid of the full revelation of any conviction of sin will, at best, bring about temporary religious relief. Transformation like the one Peter experienced, on the other hand, comes as a result of an authentic revelation in the heart accompanied by an irresistible need to proclaim it. God's Word is released and ratified from a confessed heart-belief. Salvation in Christ Jesus can't be birthed out of a forced confession but must come from a genuine repentance of the heart.

Repentance: Turn Away from and Turn Toward

Every day, we make choices to turn away from one thing and turn toward something else. And our words and our actions are huge indicators of the affections of our heart.

Our words reflect a heart of repentance. Our words often reflect our most recent passionate pursuit. It could be a movie, friend, hobby, or book. Let me explain what I mean.

When my daughter was a toddler, she would cry tears of sorrow after being caught in the act of doing something wrong. "Oops, I have been caught and now I need to smooth things over with my daddy," was the expression of her sorrow. This was not a godly kind of sorrow but one that regretted getting caught and being held accountable.

Then, as a child of seven or eight, she would come to me willingly after becoming aware that her actions were not pleasing to the Lord. She may have been selfish with a friend or may have spoken harshly and been overly critical to someone. That was pure-hearted, godly sorrow. "I am sorry," she would say. "I know it wasn't right, and as soon as I felt myself doing it, I had to say I'm sorry." Her tenderheartedness paved the way for continued growth and health in her walk with the Lord and in her relationships. "Godly sorrow brings repentance that leads to salvation and leaves no regret, but worldly sorrow brings death" (2 Cor. 7:10).

The contents of our confession and the substance of our belief act like a giant, pointing arrow. Our confession and belief represent the present position of our hearts and indicate the direction toward and the direction from which it has been turned.

Over the years, my wife and I have established a good habit of turning toward one another. When discussions become passionate and a little more vocal than they should be, we recognize the need to turn again toward one another and away from the perceived differences of opinion that have been pulling us apart. A short time may pass before this happens, but we understand the need for it to happen.

God's Word is the fuel for why we sacrificially love one another and live according to this belief. In this way, we demonstrate our love and commitment to one another. Either one of us could continue to enforce our "rightness," but in doing that, we would remain right separately instead of right with one another. Those repentances can be as simple as saying, "I'm sorry. Will you forgive me?" Our mouths confess what should be the contents of our hearts toward one another. And those words empower the reconciliation and restoration needed to keep us one.

Some Salvation Basics

Stop a minute and look at the definition of *salvation*. It helps answer this question: What does a daily, outward working of salvation look like?

Salvation is a free gift (Eph. 2:8). When we receive the free gift of salvation, we also receive a charge to be fruitful and multiply that gift. God has given us a measure of faith to release the gift of salvation, and He has poured out His grace so we may access the faith required.

Salvation can be defined as deliverance, welfare, prosperity, preservation, or safety. The Greek word for *salvation* in the New Testament is *sōtēría*. It is a derivation of the root word *sózō*, which means "to save or rescue."

That is where the term "getting saved" comes from. But salvation isn't just about a moment of rescue. First, we were all saved by what took place at the cross, not by what happened when we accepted it as a living truth for us. Yes, Christ saved (past tense) us from before the foundation of the world. Jesus was the total sacrifice from eternity past. When we confess or say yes to His saving word of truth, our condition moves from a promise given to a promise received.

Salvation isn't the end of a received promise but more like the beginning of an ongoing process of transformation. At the moment of conversion, our spirit is immediately transformed and given an explosive, glorious entrance into the family of God and the kingdom of God. The belief in our hearts and the confession of our mouths activate the dynamic truth of God's Word into our present existence.

For he has rescued us from the dominion of darkness and brought us into the kingdom of the Son he loves, in whom we have redemption, the forgiveness of sins.
—Col. 1:13–14

Therefore, if anyone is in Christ, the new creation has come: The old has gone, the new is here!
—2 Cor. 5:17

In one sense, this new-creation moment is a one-time event that moves further into our past the longer we have been saved. It is like a birthday we mark on the calendar and celebrate annually. But if we stop there, we miss out on God's plan and purpose to use us to release the fullness of His kingdom—more specifically, His lordship—in our lives now. Jesus came to give us life and life overflowing (John 10:10).

The truth of daily kingdom living means we will be safe and delivered to the lord to whom we confess with our mouth and believe in our heart. We can choose a kingdom of light and life or a kingdom of darkness. Regardless of our past profession of faith or whether our names are written in the Lamb's Book of Life, our daily salvation is released according to our confession.

The Apostle Paul's salvation verses (Rom. 10:9–10, 13) describe the combined effect of kingdom transformation. He was not prescribing a liturgical prayer or a formula to achieve it. He wasn't suggesting a one-and-done kind of event. "Saved" should be understood here as both past tense and a continuous releasing of wholeness and a saving power in the life of the believer in the present.

Jesus Christ is the One who is and was and is to come (Rev. 1:8). And He is the One who continuously makes all things new (Rev. 21:5). When we confess Jesus as Lord, He has saved us, is saving us, and will continue to save us.

CHAPTER TWO

The Law of Lordship Overview

The Power of Confession

I wrote an expanded paraphrase of Romans 10:9–10, 13 to help paint a bigger picture of how the Law of Lordship works. It emphasizes what it means to confess and live a life in confirmation of God's Word.

> The sum total of all of your utterances and actions as you live obediently out of the revelation of Jesus Christ results in a continual releasing of the complete and perfect wholeness contained in the Word of God, establishing and expanding the kingdom of heaven on earth while manifesting the perfect will of God through Jesus Christ as Lord.

The meaning of the word *confession* is not limited to a spoken acknowledgment. When we confess, it not only encompasses but supersedes spoken language. Examine this phrase: "If you confess with your mouth" (Rom. 10:9 NKJV). That means agreeing with God's truth in a verbal way. Used in this context, *to confess* means to say the same thing as or to agree. It's not only saying the same thing God says, but it's verbalizing to live it from a place of true heart-belief.

When belief is rooted in the heart, your expression comes from a place of faith, persuasion, trust, and confidence. That should confirm that whatever belief we hold is absolutely true.

This confession or agreement should be so strong that it manifests in our pursuits, our affections, and our overall manner of living. The culmination of this then forms the big picture of our confession. This understanding of confession is what either aligns with or denies the truth we are proclaiming with our human vocabulary as confession.

If we truly are to live to the praise of His glory, as Ephesians 1:12 indicates, what exactly is praising or giving glory? Is it merely a group of words from the tongue of a known human language? Does a creed or liturgical prayer accomplish this? No. Those are just part of it. What those ideas convey is much bigger.

Those words are a total life expression of the manifestation of complete agreement with God's Word. The expression of our life declares as testimony and confession. Our purposeful and obedient existence must be a declaration that corresponds to God's truth. It is a consistent and ongoing confession, not just a one-time occurrence of a spoken prayer in response to an altar call. God's Word speaks of heavens declaring, rocks praising, and all creation worshipping. Yet rocks don't speak English or Japanese or Greek; they speak the language of heaven. They speak the language of eternity. They confess by their very existence the truth of eternity that Jesus Christ is Lord of all. "The heavens declare the glory of God. . . . Day after day they pour forth speech" (Ps. 19:1–2). "The stones of the wall will cry out" (Hab. 2:11).

Confession of Jesus Christ can be summed up by demonstrated righteousness, by existing in alignment with God's truth. We can claim to be the righteousness of God in Christ Jesus, but we must also live a life that provides evidence of this truth.

This is a life in full alignment with the revelation of our true heart-belief. Obedient, sacrificial living has a voice, and that voice speaks loudly through all eternity. See how scripture confirms this. "By faith Abel offered to God a more acceptable sacrifice . . . though he died, he still speaks" (Heb. 11:4 ESV).

Our life is our confession. Our life tells a story. It testifies to our belief. It declares who is Lord and who our Savior is. Words are meaningless unless the life we live demonstrates the truth behind them. In Ephesians is the summary statement of the confirmation of and purpose behind the gift of salvation through Christ: "So that we who were the first to hope in Christ might be to the praise of his glory" (Eph. 1:12 ESV).

The Law of Lordship Overview

Often, we aren't aware when our words are not testifying of Jesus Christ in confirmation that we are living to the praise of His glory. The telltale signs can be traced back to the content of our words.

The father of lies is more than willing to release and enforce his kingdom and his kind of wholeness. Call it anti-salvation—his kind of welfare, deliverance, safety, and prosperity. He has the wisdom of the world to give you and the content of the kingdom of darkness to fill your life. "The tongue has the power of life and death, and those who love it will eat its fruit" (Prov. 18:21).

I see this manifested when I get to pray for people in church. They come down to the front of the sanctuary and ask for prayer. So I can pray with some precision and speak the Word of God over them, I normally ask, "What can I agree in prayer with you about today?" I want to listen closely and hear what their confession points to.

The content of their words tells me the struggles of their heart. They might say, "My house is in constant strife. I just want peace. Pray that I can find peace." That tells me so much. That person is convinced that peace isn't something they have access to. As a Christian, they certainly have already professed Jesus Christ as Lord, but they aren't experiencing the lordship of the Prince of Peace. So the kingdom of the Lord of peace is somehow being stolen or canceled out in their life.

Perfect peace is part of the wholeness that salvation in Christ Jesus has to offer. Peace wasn't withheld from this person when they confessed Jesus Christ as Lord. The problem is that their confession, the way they're living their life, doesn't agree with the truth of God's Word in this area. And their heart is conflicted about what to expect.

It's a tough realization, but you can't lose something you already have unless you give it away intentionally. It may be that this person said the following on a regular basis: "I'm afraid these bills are going to put us in the poorhouse. What are we going to do? I can never get a break in life. What I wouldn't give for one moment of peace around here."

In this situation, I have to wonder who is really being confessed as lord. The lord of hopelessness? The lord of never gonna happen for me? Or the mysterious magic genie who just might trade you for some peace if you give him something of value?

But if we are believers in Christ Jesus, we have already made that trade. We've repented of our self-led, sin-soaked life and traded it for His offer of redemption through His eternal sacrifice.

Peace isn't something we ever lose if we are in Christ Jesus and under His lordship. The Lord Jesus Himself spoke to the storms. He wants us to realize that the storms, while they may come, have no power to take peace from us. The peace we have in Christ Jesus, both under His lordship and because of the revelation that He is the manifestation of perfect peace, must be the primary heart confession on our lips. If not, we will struggle to live in divided kingdoms.

I know a guy who used to say every day, "Well, today is probably going to be lousy, so if anything good happens, it will be a surprise." He was thinking that if he didn't get his hopes up, he wouldn't be disappointed when things eventually did go wrong.

There was a false lord of low expectations being empowered by his words. He was confessing and inviting the "lord of the lousy day" to preside over each day. Somewhere along the way, my friend became convinced he wasn't worthy of walking in any kind of divine favor from the Lord. He wasn't trusting in the Lord with his heart. He was leaning on his own understanding. All the while, he was totally unaware of the simple matters of lordship that were operating as the result of his confession and his heart-belief.

The power of the influence of the words we receive, pay attention to, and give utterance to can't be underestimated. It's vital to know that God's Word must constantly be the biggest revelation in our hearts. God's Word must continually flow in and overflow out so there is no room for anything else.

What comes out of our mouths is the rudder that steers the ship of our focus; it is the revealer of the condition of our hearts. What we lift up, we make lord. What we confess, we make lord. What we continually speak and make room for will be the lord of our lives in the areas we release those words.

We can't annul our words by saying we were just kidding. We won't be off the hook for a careless use of words, even if popular culture has replaced the true meaning of those words with cute sarcasm, witty banter, and slang. Those words are empty words, devoid of truth and power. "But I tell you that

The Law of Lordship Overview

everyone will have to give account . . . for every empty word they have spoken" (Matt. 12:36). "For the mouth speaks what the heart is full of" (Luke 6:45).

By calling, crying out, confessing, speaking, and declaring, we are expressing both our current position and our intended position. Let me explain. When we complain, we are actually repenting from gratitude. We have renounced a thankful heart and released an ungrateful one. Because we believe what we speak, those words immediately infect our hearts and then redirect our purpose toward that end.

How we speak and how we live reflect who is governing our lives. Whoever we continually confess from the place of our heart-belief will be our lord. And whoever that lord is will supply all our needs according to the resources available to them.

Matters of lordship can be compared to any other law. Take the law of gravity, for example. Gravity is one of many laws that come to bear in the physical universe. Gravity does what it is going to do, even if we don't have the scientific jargon to explain it. Gravity is a force that affects us and everything around us.

Yet there is another law that can suspend the law of gravity. It is the law of lift, which allows airplanes to fly through the air in defiance of the law of gravity. Both of these laws are the result of other complex relationships that can be studied in the subject of physics. Like these physical laws that may stand alone or interact with one another, the Lord helped me see three simple components that work together to establish what I call the Law of Lordship.

King David spoke of God's Word as a law. David said he loved the law (Ps. 119:97). Scholars believe he was referring to all scripture he had access to at the time, which were the first five books of the Bible, called the Pentateuch. The Apostle Paul spoke about the law as a teacher (Gal. 3:24). God's Word teaches us.

When a judge is faced with a decision, that judge will render a verdict according to the rule of law. The law is the guide. What happens as a result of the law depends on our cooperation with it.

The Law of Lordship will teach us, guide us, and help us make decisions. It will influence the quality of life we choose to live. The choice is ours. The law won't change. It will continue to act as a force in our lives. Knowing more about the meaning and power of the three components that make up this Law of Lordship will help us.

The three matters aren't entirely independent. Picture them as three intertwining cords of a strong rope. The three matters have unique, individual purposes, but God has chosen to put them together in agreement with His Word to release salvation. These matters establish lordship and release salvation.

The Heart of These Three Matters

The first matter is based on who God says He is. It also means that the enemy is who he says he is. The first matter is foundational to the other two.

The second matter shows an established dependence that all His creation has on Him, a dependence that He designed to help us, not hurt us. Likewise, the second matter shows that our dependence on the enemy can easily replace our designed dependence on the Lord.

The third matter shows that Jesus desires the first two matters to work together to empower us to accomplish His will for our lives and for His glory. The first two matters are a dynamic duo that release salvation or wholeness in God's kingdom. However, the first two matters in the hands of the enemy will create a wholeness or a "saving to" the kingdom of darkness and to an allegiance to other lords.

That explains why the title of this book isn't *The Matters of the Lordship of Jesus Christ*. The title *Lordship Matters* relies on you, after a full understanding, to determine who is your lord and where is your kingdom. Our confession, our manner of living, our place of salvation, and the very stewardship of our lives are all dependent on these matters. Combined, they establish a rule of law: the Law of Lordship.

This law operates in the life of every single living soul, whether they are aware of it or not. They are matters of interdimensional importance, and they apply to the kingdom of light and to the kingdom of darkness.

Everyone confesses something. Everyone is lorded over by something or someone. We all experience a "saving to" something or someone. You will live by a set of truths that determine the lord, the confession, and the kind of saving you experience.

The Law of Lordship: Three Irrefutable Matters

1. *The name of the Lord is the nature of the Lord.*

   All the names of God in the Bible are both who He is called and what He does. His name I AM establishes this. He tells us He will never go back on His word. His word and His name are one and the same. As we declare and worship His name, His nature will not only be evident, but He will move on our behalf, consistent with His name and His nature.

2. *The nature of the Lord is our need for the Lord.*

   The needs of our hearts are the center of our belief, which guides our manner of living. At creation, God made us to need Him. We are complete when we are found in Him. The best thing for us is His nature. We don't really need material things; our true need is for His nature to fulfill our deepest desire for Him.

3. *The need for the Lord in us is the need of the Lord through us, releasing salvation.*

   When our needs align with His nature, His salvation (wholeness) will move through us. The need for who God is—to be who He wants to be in us—resonates in us and compels us to call out to Him. We worship Him, and we speak of who He is. We are His representatives on earth. So as we speak His name, His nature is revealed, which results in His saving power moving through us to accomplish His plan on earth. This isn't just salvation for us and to us; it is the cycle of salvation through us.

A simple picture would be to imagine the three matters as three ingredients of a recipe. The recipe creates God's will on the earth. The result is everything God wants to see take place through us, His people, His creation.

Because of our sinful nature, the law of sin and death says we aren't allowed to cook in the kitchen. That law tells us we will never taste and see the goodness of the Lord, that we will never share this goodness with others.

But because God stocked the pantry, created the perfect recipe by giving us free access through the sacrifice of Jesus, we can fill the earth with the most tasty, delicious, satisfying culinary creations ever. We aren't just feeding ourselves; we get to help feed and nourish our fellow believers as well as draw the unsaved into the kingdom of God.

As I navigate each of these matters of lordship, I liken it to walking around Stonehenge. I see the light and shadows of the stones interacting, highlighting and illuminating details and perspectives I could never fully appreciate from a distance.

Any individual stone at Stonehenge would be a marvel in itself, but to see them all together is a wonder to behold. The stones are difficult to experience separately because the wonder comes in their reference to one another.

The matters of lordship are a powerful truth from God's Word. Each matter is reflective and responsive to the others and together, they form a cohesive system. And that system is a powerful law for us to cooperate with as we grow in the grace of the Lord Jesus Christ.

CHAPTER THREE

The Name of the Lord Is the Nature of the Lord

You are good, and what you do is good.

—Ps. 119:68

God must be known according to what He does. God is good, and He does good. His name is good, and His nature is good. What He does is also who He is. He loves. His name is love. He is the Lamb slain from before the foundation of the world. His love is sacrificial. He is our sacrifice. Whenever the Bible says He is the God of something, it is the same as calling Him by His name. The God of all grace. The God of glory. The God of vengeance. These are not only His names, but they also reveal His nature.

His name is Lord, and His name is I AM. We need to hear this as though the Almighty is saying something like this:

> I AM LORD. And trust Me, you need Me to reveal My nature in you. You need Me to release My nature in you. You need Me to release My nature through you. I want us to do this together. I want to be with you and be your God. I will be all I want to be if you allow Me to be who I AM in your life and in your world.
>
> And it is in the context of my being LORD I AM that you will experientially know who I really am. You will speak for Me, you will declare who I AM, you will release My will and My kingdom of heaven into this fallen earthly realm, and you will partner with Me in the unfolding of My plan of redemption from before time began.

The Name of Jesus Christ as Lord I am

> *God said to Moses, "I am who I am [I will be what I will be].... I am has sent me to you."*
>
> —Exod. 3:14–15

> *Hear, O Israel: the Lord our God, the Lord is one.*
>
> —Deut. 6:4

The phrase "I am who I am" or, more precisely, "I will be what I will be," is the Hebrew word *EHYEH*. The Lord is the One who is and the One who will be. God then said to Moses to tell His people, "The Lord has sent you." That word in Hebrew is *YHWH*. The sacred divine name for the God of all creation is translated Lord or, fully expressed, I am Lord.

And in that one-word name—in Hebrew, *YHWH*, I am Lord—God gave Moses the equivalent of unlocking the genetic code, the master life force to the entire universe.

You see, it isn't just the Lord in general who is declared in Romans 10:9–10, 13. The many names of the Lord I am come into the picture. They are one and the same.

Another part of the etymology and evolution of the word *lord* can be traced back to the Old English word *hlāford*, which originated from *hlāfweard*, meaning "loaf-ward" or "bread-keeper," reflecting the Germanic tribal custom of a chieftain providing food for his followers.

> *Then Jesus declared, "I am the bread of life. Whoever comes to me will never go hungry, and whoever believes in me will never be thirsty."*
>
> —John 6:35

> *Give us today our daily bread.*
>
> —Matt. 6:11

The bread of life, Jesus Christ Lord I am, is our sole source of life. When false lords feed us, it's no wonder we tend to keep them in power. Why would your soul want to starve itself of needed nourishment? We grow needy and dependent on bread that isn't from Jesus Christ, our Lord I am.

In the Gospel of John, Jesus confirmed His identity as I AM. Jesus said He is the Bread of Life, the Light of the World, the Gate, the Good Shepherd, the Resurrection and the Life, the Way, the Truth, and the True Vine.

Calling on the Name

It is mind-blowing to fathom that in all of scripture, the Lord is identified by 956 names. When we call on the name of LORD I AM, we don't limit that to a specific list of attributes of His nature. We aren't confined to (as if this list wasn't enough) the specific references to those 956 names of LORD I AM. No, we are also speaking LORD I AM every time we speak any portion of His Word into the atmosphere.

Authentic confession of Jesus Christ as Lord will always be in agreement with His Word. Speaking His Word is equal to confessing Jesus Christ as Lord to the glory of God the Father. Every scripture, every book of the Bible, is the testimony of Jesus Christ as Lord.

I will bow down toward Your holy temple
And give thanks to Your name for Your lovingkindness and Your truth;
For You have magnified Your word according to all Your name.
—Ps. 138:2 NASB

Think about what this is saying. I will bow down, make myself low, and make sure I am fully repentant in posture and in heart attitude as I give thanks, calling His name into honor and reverence. His Word of truth is magnified over all according to His name, Jesus Christ LORD I AM. The New American Standard Bible (NASB) makes it clearer than other translations.[1]

Though these concepts may appear simple, I never saw the message so clearly before. Perhaps that is why the Lord directed me to call upon "wisdom as Lord" specifically. It was salvation to this revelation about the Laws of Lordship that resulted in my crying out for wisdom.

---

1. Other translations lead us to believe that His Word is higher than His name. That can't be possible if His name and His Word are indelibly linked. In my opinion, the translators didn't quite handle the proper language nuance in some versions of this text. The NASB I believe more accurately explains and helps us understand that His Word (according to) His name causes the dynamic releasing of His salvation through us.

The revelation of this truth, I believe, was anchored in and released by Holy Spirit wisdom. The Lord was showing me a critical piece of information about divine order. He was emphasizing that order is in all that He does. Confusion, false doctrine, error, discord, and so on all stem from wisdom-less or disordered applications of God's Word.

God has established in His Word that His relationship with us will exist as an ongoing call-and-response, not to receive salvation into the kingdom repeatedly but to release salvation to do His will continually.

The following passages are parallel to Romans 10:9–10, 13. They speak the same truth.

He will call on me, and I will answer him;
I will be with him in trouble,
I will deliver him and honor him.

—Ps. 91:15

Call to me and I will answer you and tell you great and unsearchable things you do not know.

—Jer. 33:3

The Lord knows what we don't know. And we most certainly don't know what is needed at any given time. As much as we think we know Him, we should be aware that we never will know Him enough. It's clear that He isn't going to show us what we don't know until we call on Him.

This is, again, the essence of salvation. We say, "Lord, we don't know, but You do. We repent from our short-sighted knowing. We call upon You, LORD I AM, to show us specifically who You want to be and how You want to move in these areas that are standing against the full revelation of salvation on the earth today."

Our New Name, Our New Nature

When God names something, He names us and calls us who He desires us to be. He calls us according to who we were made to be before the fall of sin corrupted our identity in Him.

God called Abraham *father* before he was a father (Rom. 4:17). He calls us how He sees us, as He has made us. He does not call us according to how we presently are. He takes our old name and nature and gives us a new name and nature. He gives us a nature that doesn't exist in our sinful condition and makes it as though it always was, just as He is. He does this when we surrender to His name and His lordship, the lordship of Christ Jesus Lord I am.

This is both a one-time event and a daily event. When we remain under His lordship, we remain in everlasting, ever-renewing newness. The old is continually leaving and dying, and the new is a continually flowing river of new life.

When you get up on the wrong side of the bed and your spouse says to you, "Well, hey there, Grumpy!" you were called by your nature in that moment. The fruit of self has risen up and hijacked your new identity in Christ.

And while we struggle through these fleshly identity crises, Jesus Christ Lord I am has none. He is entirely good and never changes. You will always be telling the truth if you say that the Lord is good. Our greatest need is to take hold of that understanding and surrender our identity in exchange for His.

Remaining in the Name of the Lord I am

Therefore, as you received Christ Jesus the Lord, so walk in him.

—Col. 2:6 ESV

We have received Christ Jesus Lord I am. We must remain under His lordship and walk fully grounded in that eternal truth if we are to remain in Him. Paul emphasizes this reality in the following verses: "For in him the whole fullness of deity dwells bodily, and you have been filled in him, who is the head of all rule and authority" (Col. 2:9–10 ESV).

In whom? In Lord I am. Our identity is supposed to come from our completeness in Him. When salvation was released under His name, Jesus Christ Lord I am, our wholeness was instantaneously given to us. Not one thing was missing.

Grace and peace be yours in abundance through the knowledge of God and of Jesus our Lord.

—2 Pet. 1:2

When Peter writes about the knowledge of God and Jesus Christ Lord I am, he is saying they are one and the same, not two separate, divine beings. He is expressing doctrinally two aspects of the Trinity to the readers of the day who knew of the Old Testament's God I am but didn't know about the new covenant that revealed forever eternal Jesus Christ Lord I am.

As we are empowered by and filled with Jesus Christ Lord I am and called by Jesus Christ Lord I am, we are fully complete in every way. Every inspired word in scripture undergirds this truth. If Jesus Christ Lord I am isn't in every part of scripture, then He isn't in any of them. All His attributes are not only synonymous with His written and translated names, but His written Word and His name are eternally connected as one.

Not only proper nouns but also other parts of speech such as adjectives, verbs, and adverbs still communicate the name and nature of Jesus Christ Lord I am. These words are used to communicate what biblical scholars convey as biblical inspiration. All scripture is the Holy Spirit, God-breathed, Word of God. Yet scripture is conveyed through flawed people in human terms through storytelling, poetry, history, and the like.

I want to examine the following scripture from an eisegetical viewpoint, which means this is more my interpretation than a biblical exegesis. "So now faith, hope, and love abide, these three; but the greatest of these is love" (1 Cor. 13:13 ESV).

My interpretation of this verse looks like this:

So now "Jesus Lord I am Faith and the author of all true faith" and "Jesus Lord I am Hope, your living hope" and "Jesus Lord I am sacrificial agape love" abide as His natures and needs in us and through us, but the activating power and the final authority of all of these is the sacrificial atoning work of "Jesus Christ Lord I am sacrificial agape love."

If we break down the word *faith* from this passage, we could independently study it as a force that is activated by love. Without faith, it is impossible to please God. Through faith and patience, promises are inherited. And on and on. These ideas are not wrong but could be misapplied to human effort, philosophy, and potentially legalistic activity.

It is easy for us to talk about standing in faith or believing God for something. It can come naturally to think a certain prayer routine or certain consistent pattern of activities equals the exercising of our faith. Philosophers might encourage us to have a little faith, and whatever life issue that troubles you will all work out in the end. Yet in reality, faith isn't a tool or vehicle we use to get what we need. The purest form of faith is letting the Lord work in us to achieve whatever He needs.

We can rest confidently in Him and let the name of Jesus as faith do all the work. He already did all the work. Jesus is the author and finisher of our faith (Heb. 12:2). He started our faith journey by what He has already done for us, and His atoning work was a completed work. He is in us both to will and do according to His good pleasure (Phil. 2:13). We can just hold tight to Him. We can just remain in Him. We can just rest in an abiding relationship with Him.

This should relieve us from breathing heavily, sweating a lot, and checking days off the calendar until our faith works. Instead, we use the measure of faith Christ has given us. That measure is equal to the fullness of who He is when we remain in Him. We can't do anything apart from Him, anyway (John 15:5). When our faith is tried, patience is perfected (James 1:3). But the beautiful thing is that our faith isn't on trial. Jesus took our sin and our shame, and He redeemed us with His great love.

Often, we overcomplicate the simplicity of the gospel and label it the deep things of God. I suggest we view this passage through the lens of Jesus Christ Lord I am Faith. "So now faith" (1 Cor. 13:13 ESV). Consider the word *faith* to mean the name of the Lord as Faithful One. The Lord I am's name is Faithful. He is pure faith. He is the force that upholds all created and living things in the universe according to the counsel of His will (Eph 1:11 NASB). Jesus Christ Lord I am Faithful. He as faith fuels us and ignites the center of our belief system, empowering us to serve Him alone.

It doesn't matter what I think about faith or what I might try to do in faith. If Christ as Lord isn't the center, it's all irrelevant. Without Jesus Christ as our mediator, we can't come to God; we cannot please Him. So without the faithful mediator and intercessor, the High Priest Lord I am, there is no pleasing God.

Now let's look at the word *hope*. Consider that it means the name of the Lord our Hope.

We could study the word *hope* as a noun or a transitive verb, something we possess and a commodity or vehicle of our soul. We could analyze it as a human attribute to be expressed. We could study the Greek language and try to interpret what it should mean for us ad infinitum. But then does hope really have any meaning apart from Jesus Christ as Lord? The revelation of Jesus Christ as Lord I am is the lens of all biblical interpretation.

It would be better to view it from the perspective that Lord I am is the God of Hope. He is the blessed hope. He is our hope. He is our living hope. There is no hope apart from Him.

"But the greatest of these is love" (1 Cor. 13:13). This verse is a gospel summary statement. It is a recap of all of Paul's writing on love. This verse is just like saying that the name and nature of Jesus Christ Lord I am Love is the dispenser necessary to release and reveal the fullness of who He is in every way and in every possible application.

If it isn't becoming clear, please understand that these matters imply that *lord* is both the position and the name. Every aspect of His name is available for us to call upon and to experience salvation into.

Translations are problematic. Even more challenges come when a language needs to be interpreted. Culture, context, and language all frame literary works in certain ways. I am contending that Jesus Christ as Lord I am is the best benchmark for any and all interpretation and application of God's Word. If the context of any passage can't connect to, conform to, and align with the truth of Jesus Christ as Lord I am, then it will likely be misapplied in some way.

I often mentor young worship leaders. I see them working hard to pursue a dream to be used on a big platform. They refer to scriptures on using God's talent and how eventually obstacles will move out of the way so their gift can become prominent. The problem with this understanding is that it takes Jesus, the humble servant who went to the cross, and uses Him as a stepping stone instead of a path to follow in His footsteps.

They have exchanged their talent as a musician or singer with the gift of God's Son, who was given to us and for us. They don't understand that sacrificing their personal ambitions is the sweet-smelling gift the Lord wants to savor. Whatever the Lord decides to do after that will bring Him glory.

They don't realize that humbly serving another team member is the greatest gift they can offer. It isn't a platform we should be hoping to get. The goal should be for our lives to be a sacrifice that will make plain the uplifted cross of Jesus and His resurrection to the highest place. The platform belongs to the Lord. He gave us this life as an opportunity to serve Him and to expand His kingdom.

They are not misquoting scripture, but I'm suggesting that they are misapplying the heart of the truth when they leave Jesus Christ LORD I AM out of the primary application.

Any Other Named Lord

Jesus is the King of kings and Lord of lords. Who are all these other kings and lords that He is king of? I put them in three categories:

1. Humans who hold position and title in the natural and physical world
2. Demonic principalities and rulers in the unseen realm
3. Anything tangible (or not so tangible) that we allow even in the slightest degree to become elevated in our lives

Many thousands of other rulers contend for the place that only the LORD I AM should fill. Let's reflect on how many of these lords may be in our lives right now. Try to identify the kind of natures that are part of your day. By natures, I mean an emotional or physical presence such as anger, turmoil, stress, depression, chronic physical sickness, disorder, abuse, regret, and more. You're looking for anything that one of the manifest names of the Lord Jesus Christ is the answer to. Then, begin calling on Him to address those issues.

For example, it may be that you have an ongoing challenge in the workplace of unfair treatment or consistently being overlooked or undervalued. We can call on the name of the Lord who is our promotion. We can surrender to the Lord who sees the hearts of humans and who holds us in the stability of His time. We could pray, "Lord, You are right and make all things right in Your time, I rest in You. You are my Lord, and I trust that You are working all things together for my good in this situation."

The second step is to evaluate if in any way, directly or indirectly, the presence is the result of your calling on the wrong names. What might that look like? Well, someone might say this:

My kids are always misbehaving, I don't expect anything else.
We are just a big hot mess, what can I say?
We're always stressed; that's how we roll.

It is good for us to acknowledge our need for the Lord and to recognize our helpless condition without Him. It's perfectly okay to admit we don't have it all together and that we are all works in progress growing in the grace of the Lord Jesus.

But most of the time, we aren't aware of the toxicity of the words we speak. Those words amount to calling out and calling upon things, ideas, investments of time, and the like that exalt themselves to a place of lordship in our lives.

I've heard people berate family members because someone kept them from seeing a favorite TV show. "I'm not happy now," they say. Then sarcastically, they say, "Thanks a lot."

The message conveyed here is that happiness comes from an hour in front of the television. Really? It might be a simple pleasure if all of our other time was well-spent and well-invested in the kingdom of God.

Here's another example. You or someone you know may have the persistent need to voice an opinion or comment on every minutia of life. What does that tell us about this person? They reject or lack self-control and strive to control the conversation. There is an absence of the fruit of the Spirit; there is the presence of an unbridled tongue. It represents a missing identity in Christ Jesus. If we can't really see Him as the Lord Jesus our affirmer, our champion, and the One who meets our needs, then of course we have to remain in control with our mouths and the comments we make.

There have been lords called upon who have been released and empowered by mouth confessions and heart-beliefs of a broken, fallen, sin-oppressed humanity for many millennia of human history.

Why do I use the phrase sin-oppressed? Because our liberty and freedom were (past tense) procured through the life, death, burial, and resurrection of Jesus Christ Lord of all. Sin is powerless to determine our eternal standing. We are no longer slaves to the law of sin and death. But we do allow ourselves to become re-entangled with the weight and snares of a sin-sick world.

In other words, we are oppressed by the enemy. Those temporary realities exist to the believer as an oppressive condition. Anyone, including born-again, saved Christians, can fall into unhealthy patterns of speaking and living that cooperate with the enemy, the counterfeiter of lords. Jesus Himself called out the devil's masquerade into the open.

The Lord Who Steals and Kills

The thief comes only in order to steal and kill and destroy. I came that they may have and enjoy life, and have it in abundance [to the full, till it overflows].
—John 10:10 AMP

The thief is who Satan is. His name is *thief*, and he is good at stealing, killing, and destroying. His name is his nature. When the thief is lord, his nature becomes our need. It becomes our nature to steal. He is all too convincing in his appeal, and he has the legal (even if only temporary) power to present himself as the real life-giver, stealing and destroying the reality that our true need for life can only come from Jesus Christ Lord I am.

The enemy of our souls who kills, steals, and destroys does so by convincing humankind that we need who he is. He will give the kingdoms of this world in exchange for worship. Any time our words agree with his ways and the ways of this world—selfishness, personal gain, greed, envy, pride, or the lusts of the flesh—we are confessing him as our lord and releasing his kingdom in our lives.

What exactly is Satan killing, stealing, and destroying? Your material goods? Did he come to make your car break down? Circumstantial setback? No. He comes to steal the identity of Lord I am, to kill the life you are meant to be living under that revelation, and to destroy the fullness of the kingdom reality that you and I should be living now. He is attempting to disrupt and destroy our revelation of Jesus Christ as Lord I am so we have no effective daily confession and witness of Jesus Christ as LORD I AM to the glory of God the Father. But Jesus Christ LORD I AM came to give us the real kind of overflowing kingdom life.

Satan wants us to think our possessions are important, our status is important, or our dreams are important. They become so important that we pursue the object of our desires instead of the only need of our heart, Jesus Christ our Lord. Our material goods are only a temporary blessing at best in this life. When we value stuff for stuff's sake, our priorities are in the wrong place.

The material possessions of life should be like seeds, surrendered back to the Lord for the purpose of growing the kingdom of God under the Lordship of Jesus. If not, our possessions will partner with the enemy and steal, kill, and destroy our true need for Jesus LORD I AM. Take a look at the bait-and-switch game going on for lordship.

And no wonder, for Satan himself masquerades as an angel of light.
—2 Cor. 11:14

You used to live in sin, just like the rest of the world, obeying the devil—the commander of the powers in the unseen world. He is the spirit at work in the hearts of those who refuse to obey God.
—Eph. 2:2 NLT

Did you notice what it says about the spirit at work in hearts? It is still our choice to obey God or disobey God. The audience here is not the unbelieving heathen. Paul is writing to the believer in Jesus Christ, the called-out saints, the church on earth. He is warning us not to let the devil work an act of disobedience against the lordship of Jesus in our hearts.

The name of Jesus is above all rule and authority, power and dominion, and every other name. Yet this reality for the time being doesn't eliminate these other authorities and powers.

Far above all rule and authority, power and dominion, and every name that is invoked.
—Eph. 1:21

The Name of the Lord Is the Nature of the Lord

We have access to a relationship with the name above all names—Jesus. When we speak His name and nature under His lordship, we release His kingdom (salvation). We must be mindful, though, that we also have the same access to all the other names, lords, and powers.

Satan is vying for our hearts. If he can win our heart space, he will work the Law of Lordship to his advantage. Satan has free access to work in the hearts of anyone who empowers him to do so.

Jesus identifies this lordship battle and describes it in the parable of the sower (Matt. 13:19–23). Instead of His Word and His name being given complete and total heart ownership, the cares of this world not only choke out the life-giving potential of God's Word, but they also produce other kinds of harvests. We, too, often share space with other lords. And those other lords have other harvests in mind.

Sometimes, when our foundation isn't in the truth of Jesus as Lord, we hear the Word of God and misunderstand what it means for us. It seems like many of the attempts to make God's Word culturally relevant to our modern context contribute to this kind of misunderstanding. Some of the great gems from Jesus's teachings are best gleaned from a first-century, historical, and cultural understanding. In Matthew 11:7[2] when Jesus mentions the word *reed*, it may well have been a veiled reference to a political figurehead of the day. Without that information, His intent in that passage could easily be made into a confusing message that the evil one snatches from our heart.

Another example might be that our reputation among peers or coworkers could hinder us from speaking out in support of a biblical worldview. In that instance, while our reputation remains solid with those around us, the reputation of Jesus will be hindered from shining through in our lives. The seeds that could be life-giving to others could be choked out by our concern for a worldly reputation. There is a subtle clue here that should capture our attention. Jesus says that those who hear and don't understand have this mixed-soil problem going on. Hearing must equal obedience. Faith comes by hearing (repentance from sin and obedient response to) the Word and hearing the Word of God.

---

2. "As John's disciples were leaving, Jesus began to speak to the crowd about John: 'What did you go out into the wilderness to see? A reed swayed by the wind?'"

The word *understand* can be flipped around to be *stand under*. When we are standing under or surrendering to the lordship of Jesus Christ Lord I am, we receive the truth of God's Word, and it produces the harvest God sent it to accomplish.

The name of the Lord isn't just a name to be recited or called out. His name is a relationship and an intimacy we are to experience constantly. To know His name is to know His nature. When we say His name is faithful, we must also know and experience His faithfulness. That comes through the course of living a life where trials and challenges rage against our profession of His name.

But what a deeply rich and rewarding journey awaits us if we continue to press deeper into the name of the Lord and experience fully all of His nature. And it is along that journey that we discover more every day how deeply we were created to need Him.

CHAPTER FOUR

Our Need: The Nature of the Lord Is Our Need for the Lord

Be fruitful and increase in number; fill the earth and subdue it.
—Gen. 1:28

God is a purposeful Creator. From the very start, He made us to be like Him. We have been created in His image and likeness. We have been charged with subduing the earth and living as procreators. Be fruitful and increase are the charges He has given us. That isn't something we figure out how to do on our own. It must be fulfilled according to the manner in which He created us and according to who He created us to be.

Think about that. He intended us to physically be fruitful *and* to use the authority He gave us to be fruit-bearing creators, just like Him. This isn't just a command to have babies. He is saying something like this to us: "Be proactive about using the life-giving, creative power I have placed in you as beings I have created in my image and likeness."

The God who made the world and everything in it is the Lord of heaven and earth . . . he himself gives everyone life and breath and everything else.
—Acts 17:24–25

For it is God who works in you to will and to act in order to fulfill his good purpose.
—Phil. 2:13

We are all created with a built-in need for the nature of our Creator to be resident, vibrant, and active within us. This is the perfect picture of the

Law of Lordship operating to release salvation, birthed in us by Jesus Christ Lord I am Salvation Himself.

The embracing of any need other than for Him as Lord I am empowers strongholds and agrees with principalities that oppose Him as Lord I am. It might sound like a semantic difference, but I have heard people pray, and I have prayed this way myself: "I take authority over you in the name of Jesus!"

Why are we taking authority? It was never taken from us. It was given to us by Jesus who has all authority. If we live in Him and move in Him and have our being in Him, then everything we speak will emanate from a place of being in Him. The enemy is rebuked and held at bay by our constant living confession of Jesus Christ Lord I am.

The truth is that all too often, we undermine this reality when we repeatedly surrender it in a flip-flop, up-and-down head game led by emotions and soul-driven responses.

Why is the enemy's resistance so strong in our lives? Why does it sometimes feel like all hell is breaking loose? Much of it is our perception. In reality, all hell isn't breaking loose. Many times, we are struggling with territories we have willingly given away. And we somehow think it has to be a battle royale to recapture them.

In one case, where Jesus was releasing salvation of His kingdom into a lame man, His approach was called into question. "Which is easier: to say, 'Your sins are forgiven,' or to say, 'Get up and walk'?" (Luke 5:23).

Our Need for Who He Is Will Release What He Does

It's an interesting question: Which is easier for me to say? "Rise and be healed" (address the symptom and work a miracle) or "your sins are forgiven" (address the root need and let the revelation of I am release salvation onto the earth)?

The lame man needed the Lord I am. He didn't need a cure. He didn't need a physician. He didn't need a supernatural miracle. Any of those other things, believe it or not, could occur apart from repentance of sin and releasing of salvation in Christ Jesus Lord I am.

We are to live and speak according to every word God speaks into us. Our hearts must exist as focused points of believing only in our Creator, His way, His plan, His Word, His path, and nothing else.

Our Flesh Keeps Us from Our True Need of I am

From the very beginning, there was an imposter who came to sow confusion about our nature, our identity, and who should be the source of our need. He came with an offer that said something like this: "You have a different nature, one of your own. You need to command your own destiny, and through your self-satisfaction, you must create and multiply and be all you were intended to be."

Because of the identity-questioning seed sown by the deceiver (Gen. 3:1), what once was a natural, unhindered authority given to us by the Lord must now journey through the cross of Jesus Christ Lord I am and become reborn to a new life. What once was a natural outflow of our need for the only one true Lord has become an ongoing spiritual battle.

Our own flesh has become the hindrance against God's greatest design for us. As long as the earth remains, until the second coming of Jesus, we will be required to participate in the cycle of laying our lives down by crucifying our flesh. And this cycle will continue to serve as the greatest mandate and call to stewardship in our lives.

By the toil that comes from being caught in a world that bears the burden of original sin, we must navigate the releasing of His kingdom. The disciples eventually faced the harsh reality of this after failing to see a demon-oppressed boy set free. Jesus made it clear that our own flesh would be a great detriment to living and releasing the kingdom of heaven on earth. "But this kind does not go out except by prayer and fasting" (Matt. 17:21 AMPC).

When our need for the Lord is stronger than the needs of our flesh, the nature of the Lord in us will prevail, resulting in freedom, deliverance, and salvation to everyone around us. We cannot say we have no need of the One who made us. We cannot ignore the need for oneness with Him and Him alone. All of who He is reflects our intended eternal state before we said yes to sin. Our need for His nature in us confronts the reality of sin's curse that works against us, a reality we seem to struggle against even after we have been born again into a new life in Christ Jesus.

Needs in the Wrong Priority

What have we become dependent upon? A routine? Foods? The investment of our time? The items we spend money on? If those things serve in a way that gives us fulfillment, they are in the wrong place. Our only need should be for the Lord.

Many people enjoy attending church and fellowshipping with other Christians. The church is the Body of Christ on earth today and is a wonderful, purposeful place for the Lord to do His work and be glorified. But if the church's activities and programs become the main object of our affection, if those things fulfill us in a way that makes us overly legalistic and protective of the routine and ritual above all else, then they have become exalted to the wrong place.

Family is a wonderful institution designed by the Lord. Yet I have seen many believers make an altar and god of the family-first idea. Many refuse to plan in a healthy, prioritized way the commitment to serve in the local church. They often make excuses for not ministering with excellence or honoring commitments to jobs and community because family comes first.

When Christ as Lord is the center, our priorities are kingdom priorities, and Jesus Christ is Lord over them all and must be evident in them and through them. As disciples of Jesus, we should walk a disciplined, prioritized life.

I suggest that the Lord can be first in every one of our priorities. And I believe that as we live for the Lord Jesus, each area of our lives will require sacrifices as our reasonable act of worship and service to Him.

What should be our first nature—to be completely whole in Him—has become divided and dismantled by the enemy of our souls. The world, our flesh, and the enemy form a three-pronged fortress of denial against our true need for Lord I am.

We struggle to feel affirmed. God loves and totally affirms us as His. Yet when our hearts cry out for affirmation from any source other than Him, we are shedding light on all the territory of our heart-soil that is still governed by the enemy.

If we don't want God's Word to be effective, all we have to do is follow the felt needs of this life to their ultimate end. We will discover a Lord who promises to meet those needs according to his nature and his name.

The god of this world will use the lusts of original sin and turn our flesh in a way that works against our eternal standing in heaven's kingdom, the realm of the Spirit of God. The enemy reveals a pattern for this in the temptation of Jesus (Matt. 4:1–10).

The temptation of Jesus lays open the battle for lordship in our lives. The enemy desires to be the source of our need. He wants to be our lord. He tempts us to use our creative powers to fulfill the needs of the flesh. Under his rule, God's Word isn't our source of life; it is a license to pick and choose scripture for our own personal gain.

Under the enemy's rule, we play a manipulative game with God, forcing His hand as we place ourselves knowingly in peril. Under the enemy's rule, we can take the pleasures of this world for ourselves to wear as a robe of splendor, exalting them above the only true Lord of all, Jesus Christ.

The enemy tries to convince us that he is who we need and that our profession of belief should be in all that he has to offer us as god of this world. He will provide us with temporary safety and satisfaction under his kind of government.

What the enemy offers when he attempts to be lord of our lives appears to be good and life-giving. But his name is his nature through and through. Like the King of kings and Lord of lords, Satan, too, has left his heavenly place of authority and forsaken all, paying a dear price to be with you for eternity.

Let's look at a few of his names: adversary, accuser, tempter, ruler of demons, wicked one, god of this world, the destroyer, and angel of light. So when it comes to our highest and best in the eyes of the Lord, Satan is our adversary.

Satan is good at manipulating our minds, wills, and emotions to work against the real plan God has for us. He is the accuser who divides us with our self-ambition so we stand against our brothers and sisters in the Body of Christ, playing the blame game and taking a victim mentality at the hands of our fellow Christians. He is the tempter, the wicked one, twisting any truth of God's Word ever so slightly for the purpose of bringing enmity between us and our true LORD I AM, Jesus Christ.

The enemy will be your "I am" every time you speak from a place that affirms need and dependence on him as the author and finisher of your faith. Our reality should be Jesus Christ, Lord I am as our only I am and as the revealer of the true needs of our hearts.

It is an eternal established truth that Satan has been defeated and that Jesus Christ is Lord to the glory of God the Father. However, it isn't a vital truth in our lives unless we come under the authority of that truth. If we don't, the reality is that we are expressing unbelief.

Unbelief is always manifest as a failure to live by the Word of God. That is the epitome of blindness. If and when we as believers operate according to the god of this age, we are no better off than the rest of the world who have yet to confess and follow Jesus Christ Lord I am. "The god of this age has blinded the minds of unbelievers" (2 Cor. 4:4).

Every word spoken or life testimony that denies the lordship of Jesus Christ honors the spirit of antichrist. The truth of this is arresting to comprehend. "Every spirit that does not confess Jesus is not from God; this is the spirit of the antichrist" (1 John 4:3 NASB).

Conflicting Lordship

The many facets, names, and natures of Jesus as Lord could go completely dishonored in our lives, and we could end up living in divided kingdoms. Many carnal Christians struggle daily because they live in kingdoms that share a mixed rule and divided territory. They are attempting the impossible. Salvation is the condition of complete wholeness to the kingdom of heaven made available under the rule of Jesus as Lord I am. Salvation isn't partly light and partly dark. It isn't contending against itself. "If a kingdom is divided against itself, that kingdom cannot stand" (Mark 3:24).

History shows humankind's predilection to walk in unfaithfulness against a monogamous covenant relationship with the one true Lord. As a result, history is full of the demonstrated fruit and demonstrated consequences of that kind of adulterous pursuit. The Lord promised consequences when we share His throne with any other gods. "Because they abandoned the Lord their God . . . and laid hold on other gods and worshiped them and served them. Therefore the Lord has brought all this disaster on them" (1 Kings 9:9 ESV).

When we walk away from His lordship, we leave the kingdom of His favor and abandon the place of His covenant blessing. Jesus made a series of powerful statements that release to us the revelation that He is both the giver of the law and the embodiment of the law and the fulfillment of every sacrifice needed for every breaker of the law, which is all of us. Jesus quotes this passage from Deuteronomy 6:4–5: "Jesus replied, 'You must love the Lord your God with all your heart, all your soul, and all your mind.'" (Matt. 22:37 NLT).

In ancient Hebrew, heart, soul, and mind were not three separate ideas. They weren't meant to be separated into exhaustive studies on what heart love should mean, what soul love should mean, and what mind love should mean. This powerful command from the law was saying that Lord I am is everything in one; He is the only God who is fully integrated as every manifestation of perfect good in all the universe.

We must, with the entirety of our integrated being, worship, serve, and live all out for Him alone. For God's chosen people, complete obedience to the law was the expression of this great command of love.

Today, we cannot love completely except by living in and through Jesus Christ as Lord. It takes Him flowing through us as love to others and back to Him as an obedient life, one of sacrificial worship.

My mind can't do that. My passions, my soul, my flesh can't do any of that. Complete love for Him must be both a response to Him and an outworking evidence in confirmation that Jesus Christ is our one and only Lord I am.

We love because he first loved us.

—1 John 4:19

If anyone acknowledges that Jesus is the Son of God, God lives in them and they in God. And so we know and rely on the love God has for us.

—1 John 4:15–16

We are driven to succeed. We become motivated by achievement or sexual intimacy outside of the marriage covenant, and those expressions are the ones that become our declarations of lordship. Our heart isn't fully settled that Jesus Christ is Lord I am, our one and only need, or we wouldn't be crying out for fulfillment by anyone else.

The more we embrace this as reality, the greater effort we can make in surrendering to the lordship of Jesus Christ Lord I am and stand against any other truth that would assault our existence. "And my God will meet all your needs according to the riches of his glory in Christ Jesus" (Phil. 4:19).

It isn't in any specific state of either lowliness or in earthly abundance that our supply is found. It isn't a stock of money, it isn't a career path, or any other earthly pursuit—none of which will matter in eternity. It is the source of our supply. Jesus told us not to concern ourselves with earthly needs. He was telling us they are distractions. He wants us to know that if we seek material fulfillment without seeking Him, material things will become lords that will offer us a different and inappropriate kind of saving. The result will be not what He has given us but what we have chosen for ourselves. "So do not worry, saying, 'What shall we eat?' or 'What shall we drink?' or 'What shall we wear?' For the pagans run after all these things, and your heavenly Father knows that you need them" (Matt. 6:31–32).

He goes on to say, "Seek first his kingdom" (Matt. 6:33). The kingdom of God or the kingdom of heaven is governed by the King of kings and Lord of lords, Jesus Christ Lord I am. So our only true need is Him. And when that becomes a reality for us, whatever He needs will be released into our now. No sweat, no extra effort, just walking in the reality of who He desires us to be—completely found in Him.

> *What is more, I consider everything a loss because of the surpassing worth of knowing Christ Jesus my Lord, for whose sake I have lost all things.*
> —Phil. 3:8

When we fully awaken to this revelation, we begin to see Romans 10:9–10, 13 bombarded throughout God's written Word. It is everywhere. It becomes a foundational reality for interpretation of scripture. God's Word consistently calls all of creation to repentance and to confession unto salvation. It can seem subtle, but this same concept is echoed throughout scripture. "Whoever dwells in the shelter of the Most High will rest in the shadow of the Almighty. I will say of the Lord, 'He is my refuge and my fortress, my God, in whom I trust'" (Ps. 91:1–2).

Our Need: The Nature of the Lord Is Our Need for the Lord

When we realize that our need is to abide in and under His lordship in every way, His names—Most High and Almighty—will be manifest as His nature in provision of solitude and safety. They become a now reality. My real need is to be in that perfect place with Him and to carry with me His presence and His power in those ways always.

My confession then becomes that He is my Lord I am Refuge, He is my Lord I am Fortress. This is my personal God, and His nature reveals these expressions of Almighty as my one true need.

When I speak in a way that affirms that, I am confessing the lordship of Jesus Christ Lord I am to the glory of God the Father. And the result is salvation.

> *"Because he loves me," says the* Lord, *"I will rescue him; I will protect him, for he acknowledges my name. He will call on me, and I will answer him; I will be with him in trouble, I will deliver him and honor him. With long life I will satisfy him and show him my salvation."*
>
> —Ps. 91:14–16

Did you catch that? He acknowledges my name. What name? The name of Jesus Christ Lord I am Salvation. When we live obediently to what God's Word says about who He is and speak that reality out of our hearts, we will release that reality against the plan of the enemy. In doing so, our true heart-need is revealed and reinforced again and again. "The name of the Lord is a fortified tower; the righteous run to it and are safe" (Prov. 18:10).

Jesus Christ Lord I am in every expression of His nature is our place of strength. The words *run to* here are like *turn to*. When we turn to something, we turn from something else. That is a picture of continual repentance of our sinful inclination and a continual turning toward His name and His nature as our true need in Him. What is the result? Salvation for us, a constant dwelling in the kingdom we have been saved to. I want to reinterpret this verse a couple times for emphasis so you see how deep and powerful it can be for us.

The name of Jesus Christ Lord I am Truth is a fortified tower. When I run toward Lord I am Truth, then Lord I am Truth is the fulfillment of my need. I won't walk in error. I won't be given to excess and abuse of doctrine. I will surrender my truth for His truth 100 percent of the time.

The name of Jesus Christ LORD I AM GRACE is a fortified tower. When I run toward LORD I AM GRACE, then LORD I AM GRACE is the fulfillment of my need. I walk in wholeness against condemnation. I am surrounded with grace like a shield. I live graciously, I give graciously, and I receive graciously. The sharing of my faith is effective in every good word and work because my only true need is for Him.

Is this becoming clearer? When we can see God's Word in action this way, then each power-packed passage in the Word of God becomes an explosive chain reaction just waiting to be released.

In a sin-fallen world, we need peace. LORD I AM PEACE is salvation to a world in need of peace. Because His name is Peace, our need for peace is revealed. Without Him, our best efforts are still chaos. A passage from the Psalms shows us a cry we should continually release that says You made me. I don't know enough about what I should need of myself, but surely as my Maker, You know better, and You are the answer. "Your hands made me and formed me; give me understanding to learn your commands" (Ps. 119:73).

Can you see here how asking for understanding is equal to calling out to Him? It's calling on the LORD I AM to be wisdom and revelation to us. The world that is lost without Jesus is need-focused. "Give me what I need," they say, "or I will take what I need." We are not to be like them. We aren't to be need-focused or need-driven. We are to be salvation-in-Christ-Jesus-focused. He is our need. He knows our need for Him will take care of everything else. "Do not be like them, for your Father knows what you need before you ask him" (Matt. 6:8).

As long as we identify as being His, we look to Him to be the true source of our need. The more of Himself He reveals to us, the more we become aware of our need for Him.

We have a built-in need to know our Maker, our Creator. We were created to know Him and be known by Him. The expression of our need reflects who we need. It is a promise that Jesus Christ LORD I AM desires to be the fulfillment of our need.

What does it look like when this isn't a known reality? The opposite of everything I have written here becomes true. See what Jesus said about this. "Because you are unable to hear what I say. You belong to your father, the devil. . . . there is no truth in him . . . for he is a liar and the father of lies" (John 8:43–44).

Jesus called out the religious crowd for who they really represented. Their need was to be religious. They spoke from that place continually. That identity was not from Jesus Christ LORD I AM but from Satan, the lord of this world, the father of lies.

The enemy wants to keep a firm hold on all the unsurrendered heart territory in the lives of every believer so we will never fully release the gospel in this age. The enemy is anti-gospel. He is the false news, the counterfeit good news.

> *I will extol the LORD at all times;*
>   *his praise will always be on my lips.*
> *I will glory in the LORD;*
>   *let the afflicted hear and rejoice.*
> *Glorify the LORD with me;*
>   *let us exalt his name together.*
>
>   —Ps. 34:1–3

Think about these verses like this: The cry of our heart-need forms our constant confession. Our constant confession points to and glorifies our Lord. But who is getting glory? Who is being worshipped?

This kind of extolling most certainly will resonate and stir up a message of deliverance to those around us. But to what state of wholeness are we calling out into the world and drawing others to join?

Remember matter number one: His name is His nature. And as a result, matter number two: His nature is our need. When we speak of Him, we release what He needs, and we empower His ability to establish His will and His kingdom on earth as it is in heaven. His name can and should be released and declared whenever His Word speaks of His name as Lord. "The LORD is my shepherd, I lack nothing" (Ps. 23:1).

Whoever the lord is, he will lead and guide you to his place of provision. Every name and nature of whatever lord you worship will lead and guide you to the greatest fulfillment of the kingdom of that lord.

Where there is a lack of peace, turmoil, and trouble, the lord of fear is leading, guiding, and providing. Where peace, assurance of eternal purpose, and divine love are present, then Jesus Christ Lord I am is being confessed out of an intimate abiding need. His name is His nature, and His nature is what (who) I need, and whatever He needs from me, He will become in me and release through me.

A relationship with Jesus Christ Lord I am is a partnership. It is a covenant relationship. He has done His part, but He is also going to continue to interact with us, speak to us, rebuke us, correct us, reveal to us, and move through us.

It is up to us to extend faith and corresponding action daily, to walk intentionally, and to live out our part of the relationship. It's not salvation by works but a faithful stewardship on our part that manifests as a working out of the inward work. This is faith with corresponding action as an obedient lifestyle to the Word of God.

His name is His nature, and His nature is my only true need. When I declare and confess His name out of my great need for Him and begin to magnify His name as Lord, I receive the wholeness and completeness I need from Him according to His Word. I not only was made whole (past tense) in eternity, but I am continually being made whole now (present tense).

My spirit was instantaneously made whole, but my soul (my mind, will, and emotions) needs renewal. It needs to experience ongoing renewal birthed from a constant revelation followed by intentional surrender on my part to His lordship alone.

When I become aware of this, I can embrace a fuller understanding of the need to reinforce and release with the confession of my mouth the eternal truth of my eternal standing so it comes alive into my current, temporary state.

The Word says my state is completely whole in every area. My circumstances in the natural are contending against my eternal standing and pressuring me to believe in and confess my circumstances as my saving reality.

Our Need: The Nature of the Lord Is Our Need for the Lord

All we need is all who God is. It may seem like we need food, clothing, or shelter. Those are felt needs, and, yes, they are realities of our physical life on earth. But the greater truth is that the Lord is our first need. As we allow His nature to be the source of our need-seeking, He can operate as Lord of our lives. He will then be exalted and lifted up to the place He belongs.

When we place Him where He rightfully belongs, we will walk in a place of peace and rest that is a deeper kind of fulfillment than anything the material possessions of this world can offer.

CHAPTER FIVE

Releasing Salvation: The Need for the Lord in Us Is the Need of the Lord through Us

The matters of lordship convey the idea that salvation is not just a one-time event but also a cyclical process. Vital to that process is the death of self, followed by a coming alive to something that wasn't alive in us in our lost and sinful state.

We literally die and are born again. Whatever we put to death will make room for new life to spring up in its place. Whatever is fed grows, and whatever is deprived of nourishment will die.

In the kingdom of God, self-denial, surrender, and sacrifice are the seeds and the nourishment necessary for kingdom life. Conversely, in the kingdom of darkness, self-promotion, selfish ambition, worry, strife, obsession with daily provision, and more are the seeds and nourishment for a life that works against the kingdom of God.

During my prayer time in the car on those long commutes, what I cried out for, specifically *who* I cried out for, was Jesus LORD I AM. I was doing that because His Word was the greatest revelation of my heart. This wasn't a result of something I did when I was six years old on the concrete front steps of my childhood apartment home and asked Jesus into my heart and repented of my sins. No, this was the result of a daily, fresh, intentional deposit of the Word of God in my life, the Word Jesus LORD I AM Himself.

The Lord was pouring into me a response to my call. He was saving me. Not for the first time. He was showing me the ongoing release of salvation that occurs because of the Law of Lordship. He was doing that to be able to release the kingdom through me. The Lord was giving to me what He wanted from me. He was imparting to me what He wanted to do through me.

When I call, He answers, and He speaks and calls me to be obedient to release every facet of His name and His nature through me. When this takes place, there isn't room for me to give up any of my heart "real estate" to other beliefs and other lords. It must be a total and unconditional heart surrender.

Because God desires all people to come to a saving knowledge of Him, we stand as facilitators of that. The Bible says we have been given the ministry of reconciliation, which is the result of the Law of Lordship in action. "And he has *committed to* us the message of reconciliation. We are therefore Christ's ambassadors, as though God were making his appeal *through us*" (emphasis added) (2 Cor. 5:19–20).

I was amazed when I started comprehending in a greater way that who He is addresses the salvation of all things with such specificity. He is a multi-faceted, multi-expressive, multidimensional God. The fullness of the godhead—Father, Son, and Holy Spirit—is contained in the person of Jesus and in the expression of His lordship.

When we call, He answers, but it isn't a static, one-way message back to us. He responds by releasing wholeness, salvation, and all of the kingdom of heaven so they will be released through us into the earth.

A Different Lord, a Different Kind of Saving

The release of wholeness through us is the cycle of life that our enemy wants to corrupt. He wants to use that cycle of life and corrupt it so he can declare his lordship and bring himself glory. Satan, the enemy and counterfeit of everything, capitalizes on God's irrefutable Word by utilizing it to build the kingdom of darkness. How can he do this? It's simple.

God can't change who He has made us to be. He won't take back what His Word says. He has made us in His image and likeness as living, creative beings. But God also created us to be creators. He made us like Him.

Through wisdom, God by faith spoke creation into being. Still today, whenever His Word is spoken in faith, it creates (releases) His will. So we, too, can in wisdom, by faith, speak creation into being. As long as it is His Word we speak from a revelation of His Word in our hearts, we will create (or release) the fullness of His kingdom. We were made to release salvation.

Releasing Salvation: The Need for the Lord in Us

However, if Satan can get us to believe and speak out against the Word of truth, then we will create his world. If it isn't the pure Word of God we are speaking, it is the word of this world. When the god of this world, Satan, the counterfeiter's word is what we speak, then we will create his world. The enemy successfully hijacks the principles of God's Word and uses those against us.

In the earlier example I gave about my daughter calling on me, it is easy to see the Law of Lordship working when we literally call out that way. But there is another way that doesn't appear so literal.

We need only speak the Word of God or speak in any way that confirms the truth of God's Word. When we become aware of this need to speak life from the Word of God, we will begin to see the world around us as potential wholeness. Potential life in Christ Jesus will burst forth all around us when our words align with His truth.

I am convinced that when God looks at the fallen world through the sacrifice of His Son Jesus, He isn't looking at brokenness. He isn't wringing His hands over the mess we created. He sees redemptive purpose in everything. And He has given us His nature so we will cooperate with Him in continuously calling all broken things back to wholeness.

My house tends toward chaos. My garage and my basement are screaming at me, "What a mess! How can you think straight in all this clutter?" Then I drive to work on the angriest highway in the world, the New Jersey Garden State Parkway.

The furious flow of traffic and the honking-get-out-of-my-way pressure says, "Live life under stress and run like crazy to get to the next thing, or you might miss out!" My social media feed says, "Everyone else is living their best life; can't you tell by how perfect all the pictures are and see all the comments and followers they have?"

Yet the truth in God's Word speaks of a peace that can be mine that the world can't give. His Word speaks of steps that can be ordered and consistent as I follow Him. Didn't Jesus look at a dead girl and tell all the mourners she was only sleeping? (Luke 8:52). What was He doing there? "The God who gives life to the dead and calls into being things that were not" (Rom. 4:17).

He desires us to call dead things to life, unsaved things to a state of wholeness. How can we do this? By calling on the name of the Lord I am. And when we do, His Word promises that He will respond and be the solution, the peace, the healing, the justice, the miraculous, the provision, the sovereign solution in response to our calling.

When this is our understanding, we start to see brokenness, not as a problem we can fix but as salvation waiting to be released in us and through us.

He hears and responds to our confession of heart-belief when we call. If we truly believe He alone is the answer, if we repent from our dependence on any other god and call on Him, He releases wholeness to the area in need. Understanding this has dramatically changed the way I pray.

The simplest way to explain it is that we are to discipline ourselves to call on the solution, not to call out the problem. He already knows the problem. He knows that wherever there is the absence of His name, His nature, and His lordship, there is a problem. And the problem has already been taken care of by Him. Salvation in Christ Jesus is the solution to every perceived problem.

Not only do we die and get reborn in Jesus Christ, but He is literally alive in us, and we become alive in Him. It isn't we who are alive, but He who is alive in us. And He desires to be fully present in us so He can minister through us. "I have been crucified with Christ and I no longer live, but Christ lives in me" (Gal. 2:20).

Christ as Lord I am Salvation must be the source of our life, giving light and flowing like a fountain from within our very being.

For with you is the fountain of life; in your light we see light.
—Ps. 36:9

For in him we live and move and have our being.
—Acts 17:28

Our hearts and lives are vessels to be used. As we live and breathe, we will be a conduit, a releaser of some kind. The Lord desires for us to be used for His purposes. But the enemy wants that as well.

Releasing Salvation: The Need for the Lord in Us

At our confessed heart-belief, the enemy will attempt to live in us and operate through us. Does that mean he takes us over and possesses us? No. Not everybody is demon-possessed. Yet most of us partner with the enemy and cooperate with his agenda way more than we are willing to admit. Satan will persist in manipulating and buffeting every part of our mind, will, and emotions that we give him access to.

We end up willfully living and moving and having our being in partnership with the enemy instead of in Jesus Christ. Paul speaks of finding a law in operation. He didn't call it the Law of Lordship, but the Law of Lordship was present in his struggle. "For what I want to do I do not do, but what I hate I do . . . it is no longer I who do it, but it is sin living in me that does it" (Rom. 7:15, 20).

In this passage, the law of sin and death was actively working the soil of Paul's heart and attempting to produce fruit. Paul admits his inability to conquer and overcome this law. But in Romans 8, he writes of the beautiful power of life in the Spirit that is activated and empowered by Jesus Christ LORD I AM. "Therefore, there is now no condemnation for those who are in Christ Jesus, because through Christ Jesus the law of the Spirit who gives life has set you free from the law of sin and death" (Rom. 8:1–2).

Look how the truth applies to salvation in Christ Jesus. God the Father sowed Jesus into the earth as seed—the seed of promise, the Word of God, the everlasting one. Jesus, the Word, the seed that fell to the ground and died, resurrected to life.

> *Unless a kernel of wheat falls to the ground and dies, it remains only a single seed. But if it dies, it produces many seeds. Anyone who loves their life will lose it, while anyone who hates their life in this world will keep it for eternal life.*
> —John 12:24–25

We repeat and reinforce this eternal truth every time we invite Jesus as His name and His nature to be Lord, confessed as crucified, buried, and resurrected to life everlasting. When we confess that, we die again; we crucify the flesh and the pursuit of the flesh, and we continually make entrance for the life-giving power of resurrection on earth today. This idea summarizes the process of releasing salvation.

Jesus Lord I am is fully integrated. His Word is complete and whole in its entirety. He is the Word, and He is self-confirming and self-revealing in an infinite number of ways. Every scripture supports every other scripture. All of them flow out of who He is as Lord I am.

By way of example, let's look at the topic of suffering. That we are to endure suffering is a biblical truth. We aren't promised a life without pain. Some sufferings are expected, and the Lord delivers us from some. If we zero in on the truth of suffering to the exclusion of the promise of miracles or the promise of peace, we may begin to only expect suffering as a way of life and miss the big picture of God's promises in other areas. If we do that, we will have disintegrated the integrity of God's full message.

The Lord Provides What He Needs to Release Salvation

When a king needs something, he instructs a servant to fetch it. In the earthly realm, the servant has no choice but to willingly obey the king's command. If the Lord needs it, He will supply it. "If anyone says anything to you, say that the Lord needs them, and he will send them right away" (Matt. 21:3). So whatever we are praying for, this is the measurement of the will of God, that He answers every single prayer we ask when we ask according to His will. "If we ask anything according to his will, he hears us. And if we know that he hears us—whatever we ask—we know that we have what we asked of him" (1 John 5:14–15).

I interpret these verses to mean that as we believe (live by the name of the Lord I am Jesus Christ, the Son of God) we have eternal life (salvation) in affirmation and confirmation of our constant declaration, as well as in prayer by asking (confessing, agreeing with His Word according to His will), we experience wholeness.

Our wholeness or salvation is His ultimate will for us. His will aligns with and confirms the prophetic revelation of His Word, which will always declare that Jesus Christ is Lord. Always.

Jesus Lord I am Wisdom (wisdom first from His Word) gives clear instruction as to kingdom need. And as we live obediently under His lordship as our only true need, then everything that is required to release salvation gets propelled toward us as though someone turned on a giant super magnet.

Letting Our Needs Hinder His Need

We tend to conform to the object and focus of our attention. I have noticed that if something catches my attention as I drive down the road, I find it difficult to keep the car going in the right direction. The distraction literally steers me off course.

When my daughter spends too much time watching a certain movie, our whole world becomes a creative adventure from that movie. She likes the movies where dragons are trained and become like pets. We make dragon pancakes, we speak with a Scottish accent, and we even talk about writing a script for the next dragon sequel. Her focus becomes our world.

The aspects of life we make the biggest deal about can tend to take over. It may be wedding plans, shopping for a prom dress, or losing weight. But if we aren't careful, those momentary pursuits will become the foundation for a self-reinforcing belief system. Obsessing over these pursuits will become a need for us.

We might, for example, establish a codependency on being needy. We find it safe and predictable to make a list of needs, set them as prayer goals, communicate them with as many people as possible, and watch how God responds to those needs. That isn't wrong, and it totally works with a loving God who hears our prayers and moves in response to those requests.

But there is something about this obsessive asking that has always troubled me. It can create a what-do-I-need mentality instead of a what-does-the-Lord-need mindset. If I get up in the morning and start by asking myself what my needs are, I might think, "Well, I need my bills paid," or "I could use a little less stress in my life." Then I might think about consulting the Bible or asking "Dr. Jesus" what He would prescribe for that day to meet my needs. There isn't anything intrinsically wrong with that, but a different approach might be more right.

The focus could be shifted in light of the Law of Lordship and how it works, either for us or against us. If we stood under the revelation that Jesus LORD I AM is who we need and that He is in us and that we can be fully alive in Him, then we would see a greater manifestation of His kingdom and His will in our immediate spheres of influence.

If I was truly embracing and walking in this understanding, I wouldn't consult what I see to determine what I need. I wouldn't take the temperature of the room. I would, instead, get into the presence of the Lord I am, and together, we would set the climate for kingdom salvation to be released.

I wouldn't check with my emotions or my wife first. I wouldn't watch the news to see what I should pray about. I wouldn't flip through a concordance to determine what part of God's Word I should declare today that focuses on the challenges I became aware of. That would be like a physician doing a differential diagnostic based on symptoms so a prescription could be written to relieve a symptom.

Much of modern medicine isn't curative; it is primarily pain and symptom mitigation. In contrast, salvation isn't a diagnostic prescription. It is the perfect state of wholeness against which everything else attacks and attempts to break apart and destroy.

Salvation is fully equipped to stand up against any lie from the enemy that would contend for our wholeness. Salvation should be our reality, and whatever isn't whole is what has been taken from us. This condition is a temporary reality that's fighting heaven's eternal reality. We are to release salvation through us to affirm our state of being in Him, surrendered to and under the authority of His lordship.

A Lord-Need-Focused Prayer Life

Instead I might start my day by speaking out of my divinely created need to be whole and one with my Creator. I could have a conversation with myself and say, "Welcome to another day where you will have absolutely no say whatsoever about what takes place. You aren't allowed to comment, observe, or complain about anything—just be quiet. Flesh, you aren't speaking salvation to another kingdom; I will be speaking salvation under the lordship of Jesus Christ Lord I am."

I might then talk to the Lord I am about how much I need Him to be who He is today. I might just call on Him and cry out in desperation. I might confess this from my heart:

Lord, be in me who You need to be today to fulfill Your plan on earth.

I am calling on You, and I am wholly trusting in the completeness of who You are in every way.

Right now, I am putting the flesh under, I am killing all desire to be personally fulfilled so the dead things You and I come across today can spring to life as we encounter them.

Lord I am, I surrender to all the boundaries of Your kingdom; it is a safe and bountiful place for us to dwell together. I will have no other gods. I will declare no other lords today.

I might just get really excited knowing that whatever is going to take place, I don't need to call on the god of worry and begin giving him any heart-belief space by talking about the problem.

The gods that try to take the place of Jesus as Lord in my life may be different from the gods that contend for the throne of your heart. Most likely, we share some common challenges. It may be the lord of self-defense and self-justification for all our actions. Maybe it is a lord of affirmation from unhealthy or ungodly sources. It may be the challenge of emotional eating. It might be lavish, out-of-control spending.

The idea is that we live in every way a pre-filled, whole life abiding in Him constantly. Looking at the world around us not as a deficit to overcome or a dark abyss with a million and one things to try to overcome. But it is a place where we carry peace and strength as we live under His lordship, denying all other claims to the throne of our life. We could rather walk in a state of being completely whole in Him and allowing Him to flow through us in harmony with every other believer as we are living the called-out existence as the church.

We aren't living as though problems and challenges don't exist. But the greater truth, the real truth, is that those challenges aren't our needs. As soon as they present themselves as our needs, we give them authority they don't have to dictate our responses and our confessions over every other area of our lives.

In America, the established norm is pretty excessive. We have high-end coffee shops on every corner and instant gratification in the palms of our hands with smartphone technology. Many churches cater to our every whim the minute we walk in the door so we will feel comfortable, and they meet our ever-demanding need for Wi-Fi and visually stimulating environments. All those things are nice, but we don't need them.

Our true heart-need is in Him and for Him to be Lord. Then all of who He is will address those issues before we can make a big deal out of them. We won't let anything that is not Him become Lord I am to us.

I watch the news, probably too much. And what is apparent is that much of who the Lord is seems to be missing from our political dialogues. Salvation is missing from our cultural obsessions and celebrations.

Aware of this, I have a choice to make. I could sit and talk about it. I could Facebook rant about it. I could get politically active about it. But unless Jesus Christ as Lord I am is the One doing the speaking and releasing, I have done nothing worth eternal value. The wise course of action and what the Lord has revealed to me about lordship is that I can call on the name of the Lord I am and allow Him to save.

For example, I might pray along these lines: "Lord, would You bring to justice and bring to light, according to Your name and Your Word, all that is suffering from lack of wholeness in this situation? Would You move in the hearts of humanity and allow righteousness to be exalted in every expression of our leadership in this society? Convince, convict, move, and align all that is out of order and out of place, all that is dysfunctional."

I could focus my confession on calling on the only answer. And I have been doing just that. It's not that I am the model of perfection in this discipline, but I am aware of my need to continually grow in it as I press forward to pray in this manner.

Not only do I pray according to God's Word as an expression of calling on the Lord, but I speak out and declare praise and worship as a way of calling on the Lord. I could begin to cry out before Him like this:

I give place to Your authority and Your mind in this matter, Lord.

I worship You as mercy, as grace, as love, as forgiveness of sin.

I thank You and praise You for being so kind that You lead us to repentance. I make myself low, I humble my thoughts, my mind, my opinions on the subject and exalt Yours. I repent, and I speak repentance on behalf of those who aren't mindful of You and Your greater purpose and Your greater calling to salvation.

I have found this to be a fruitful and effective way to pray and worship. The Lord has promised to respond to the offering of thanksgiving and praise in our words and in our actions. While He does hear every prayer and cry, He hasn't promised to move on our behalf in response to our complaints, our selfish desires, our misunderstandings, our emotions, or the idols of our hearts that refuse to acknowledge Him as Lord.

On the other hand, if we magnify Him as Lord I am, He will be released to manifest the fullest expression of who He is—every time we call out in agreement with who He is. "Those who sacrifice thank offerings honor me, and to the blameless I will show my salvation" (Ps. 50:23).

There is that word again: *salvation*. All of the ritual sacrifices under the old covenant were types and shadows of the manifest expression of Jesus Christ Lord I am. Because we come to God through Jesus as the fulfillment of the necessary sacrifice, He is released as salvation in us and through us. This verse tells us as we sacrificially speak according to Jesus Christ Lord I am, salvation is revealed.

The repentance of our sin and our agreement with His Word release salvation. That is the whoever-calls-on-the-Lord part of the Law of Lordship in action. And it is echoed again in the book of Hebrews. "Let us hold unswervingly to the hope we profess, for he who promised is faithful" (Heb. 10:23).

Holding unswervingly, confessing continually, declaring in agreement, releasing wholeness to the kingdom under His lordship—that is what is taking place, calling what isn't whole to be made whole according to Jesus Christ Lord I am. "Through Jesus, therefore, let us continually offer . . . for with such sacrifices God is pleased" (Heb. 13:15–16).

Lord-Need Prayer Releases Lord-Need Action

I am not the solution to society's condition brought on by sin and the fall of humankind. I cannot fix a homeless person, and I cannot give them a home that will meet their ultimate need for Jesus Christ as Lord. But I can begin to call upon the name of the Lord I am as the Rest-Giver, the Comforter, the Healer to be released into the situation that is before me.

As I cry out to Him, He will begin to release the wholeness required in that specific arena of brokenness. As He does that, my perspective and attitude will begin to come into alignment for His glory. Even circumstances will change. Closed doors will open. Long-time barriers to growth will be lifted. How it all happens, I don't know, but the Lord I am has promised to go into action. And as I faithfully steward what He is releasing, it might look something like this.

He may release a plan for me to partner with others to meet the physical needs of the homeless for food, for clothing, and for shelter as a reflection of His saving power. His lordship will begin to resonate in me in a way that is evident to others.

My sacrifice in practical ways will be released from a belief in my heart that the Lord is not only my true need but that, as a result, He is who is needed in this situation. That is the right order in the kingdom. That is not doing something to be seen or to be saved, but it is humbly being used to release salvation as a response to my calling on the Lord.

The Word of God can't grow in an unsurrendered heart. The Word can't bring a harvest if it can't be planted as a seed. So where there is no seed sown, no fruit can grow. The more we make Him Lord and proclaim Him as Lord, the more we need Him as Lord. As we give Him more and more authority, we get more and more of His authority. As we proclaim Him as abundance, strength, provision, wisdom, healing, and direction—as we proclaim Him as those things as Lord—we participate in the outpouring of Him as those things in our lives.

But Jesus Christ Lord I am is the only way of salvation. He is the only One who has taken away our sins and restored us to wholeness back into the kingdom of heaven.

When we seek first the spirit of wisdom and revelation of I am, there comes a precise way to walk in the authority of Jesus as He flows through us as a release of His salvation.

It is backward to look to areas in our lives that appear to represent needs and then pray with all our might that He meets those needs—like a friend who would give us a gift or as a wealthy person who would give us money. Does He love us so much that He still responds to us when we ask and pray that way? Absolutely.

Because of our persistent asking, He will always respond. For me, it seems that our passion and persistence could be focused more powerfully toward knowing the Provider, toward surrendering and yielding under the LORD I AM of all we need. Under Jesus Christ LORD I AM, life runs completely contrary to the way we are used to.

I believe we are not designed to merely seek provision, nor are we created just to seek the answers to our most perplexing questions. I believe we are given life by the Spirit of the Almighty so we can live in order to seek Him—to seek Him with all our hearts. The paradoxical nature of this is that we must totally surrender to Him as Lord in every area before we can experience the more personal intimacy of His fatherhood and His nearness as we feel and sense companionship or friendship. He is Lord before He is any of those other titles. If He isn't Lord, He cannot be any of the others. "Trust in the LORD with all your heart and lean not on your own understanding; in all your ways submit to him, and he will make your paths straight" (Prov. 3:5–6).

As we submit and surrender to LORD I AM, whatever quality of life that is needed, His name as Lord and His nature as Lord have been established to divinely order all areas of our life rightly. Physical areas, emotional areas, logistical areas, relational areas, spiritual areas—all of them will be ordered rightly when we submit and surrender to LORD I AM.

The LORD I AM PEACE determines peace for us. When He is Lord, whatever way He leads will be the way of peace. When the LORD I AM WISDOM is Lord, we will remain on the path of wisdom—the straight path, the right path.

A journey in life that is turbulent, full of challenges and obstacles, will always be the right road and the right path when He is LORD I AM and if LORD I AM SHEPHERD has directed us there.

The most insidious sin (missing the mark and true purpose of God) and the most reprobate and totally carnal mind-set, completely calloused to the truth of God's Word, is brought about when creation is exalted over the Creator.

When our human grasp of the Almighty becomes our primary path to navigating our relationship with Him, we are in trouble. We were created to know better.

> *Because, although they knew God, they did not glorify Him as God, nor were thankful, but became futile in their thoughts, and their foolish hearts were darkened. Professing to be wise, they became fools.*
> —Rom. 1:21–22 NKJV

The manifold wisdom of God is released and made manifest in Christ Jesus our Lord. The only way to walk in the will of God in the kingdom of God is to hallow, exalt, or magnify the name of the Lord.

> *His intent was that now, through the church, the manifold wisdom of God should be made known to the rulers and authorities in the heavenly realms.*
> —Eph. 3:10

When we magnify the Lord by calling on Him as the only wise God, we rightly agree with this verse. All rulers and authorities in the heavenly realms have been served notice that the mystery of the ages has been made plain. The authority of Jesus as Lord—past, present, and future—has been declared. "On his robe and on his thigh he has this name written: KING OF KINGS AND LORD OF LORDS" (Rev. 19:16).

When Satan brought about the fall of humankind in the garden, he used his nature to present a false need to Adam and Eve. Original sin is the anchor of accepting a false salvation given by a false lord.

When the devil tempted Jesus, he distorted the truth of God's Word to appeal to the base needs of a potentially flesh-led life. Worship me, and you can really be free, he taunted Jesus. He was trying to create a need for something other than the Word of God, the Word of life. He had anti-salvation to offer.

Conversely, the Lord God Almighty has given us His divine nature. He has given us everything we need for life and godliness. Our spirit was created to know Him perfectly and intimately, to experience Him as the fulfillment of our need.

Doing the Works without Being Known by the Lord

Unfortunately, we know Satan has successfully replaced the one true Jesus Christ LORD I AM in the lives of many of those who are actively doing kingdom work in His name. Satan does that because people get lost chasing after the manifestation of power and authority in this temporary life in order to accomplish religious works.

They walked away from knowing and willingly obeying the will of God, which always acknowledges and glorifies Jesus Christ as Lord to the glory of God the Father. They ignored the totality of the Word of God that should have been released under the surrender of the lordship of Jesus. "Not everyone who calls out to me, 'Lord! Lord!' will enter the Kingdom of Heaven. Only those who actually do the will of my Father in heaven will enter" (Matt. 7:21 NLT).

We have a deep need to pursue a restored relationship with our Lord, a relationship that we have willfully destroyed by embracing our sinful condition. We are mistaken if we approach the Lord for any other reason than to know Him and be completely known by Him. Only out of being known by Him can the manifest outworking of the perfect will of the Father flow.

This idea deepens the meaning of what is supposed to take place when we call on the Lord and when we confess Him. The kingdom of heaven is eternally released in its fullness, not when we do things according to a formula or a step-by-step process. It is released when we are known and approved by Him through Jesus Christ as Lord.

> *On judgment day many will say to me, "Lord! Lord! We prophesied in your name and cast out demons in your name and performed many miracles in your name." But I will reply, 'I never knew you. Get away from me, you who break God's laws.'*
> —Matt. 7:22–23 NLT

We are too self-righteous if we think merely attending church is equal to fully keeping His Word. Jesus speaks to us in the book of Revelation about works He approves and works He does not approve.

In the Gospels, Mary and Martha demonstrate the priority of the Lord's values. He desires us to be in His presence and be filled with His heart and passion so we can go and do in His power. He isn't so much approving of our tendency to serve Him through works, especially if it gets in the way of spending time with Him. Going through the motions of ministry in His name isn't the same as remaining in Him and allowing Him to pour out His miraculous works through us.

I wonder whether the people He will say He never knew are those who had success in supernatural manifestations but failed to completely know Him and honor Him in the weightier matters of the law.

I wonder whether many of us are attempting to live life in the arena of the prophetic and the miraculous but guilty of failing to obediently surrender completely to the Lord in every other area. When we allow our flesh and our soul's desires to speak from the abundance of our hearts, we empower, enforce, and release every other ruling faction against the kingdom of God.

These other powers and names haven't been blocked from having access to creation. They are readily available to respond when called upon and will be empowered by our confession.

Remaining in the Lord: A Weapon against the Flesh

For the weapons of our warfare are not carnal but mighty in God for pulling down strongholds, casting down arguments and every high thing that exalts itself against the knowledge of God, bringing every thought into captivity to the obedience of Christ, and being ready to punish all disobedience when your obedience is fulfilled.
—2 Cor. 10:4–6 NKJV

Take a second look at these verses. Are these weapons attacking Satan and the gates of hell? Indirectly, I suppose they are since the enemy uses our mind, will, and emotions as his primary arsenal. But more directly, these weapons are made ready for us to destroy our own willful disobedience and our own uncontrolled imaginations that stand against allowing Jesus to be in full authority and governance of our lives.

Walking through a life disciplined to the lordship of Jesus means waging war against our own wayward thoughts and imaginations. It is through repentance, or turning toward God away from sin, that Jesus remains Lord and that His kingdom of wholeness can flourish. "The Lord has established his throne in heaven, And his kingdom rules over all" (Ps. 103:19 NKJV).

God's throne is over them all. The name of Jesus as Lord and the name, attributes, expression, and nature of the Lord who is declared and surrendered to as Lord will supersede and have dominion and rule over all else. Those thrones and powers only exist because He exists, and all are at His disposal for His eternal redemptive purpose. "For in him all things were created: things in heaven and on earth, visible and invisible, whether thrones or powers or rulers or authorities" (Col. 1:16).

For the wages of sin is death, but the gift of God is eternal life in Christ Jesus our Lord.
—Romans 6:23

The wages of sin is literally death—death to any part of your life that you allow to exist in the kingdom of Baal (any false god) or any expression of lord that isn't an attribute of Yahweh, Adonai, or Jehovah, Jesus Christ Lord I am.

The Apostle Paul wrote that eternal life is found in Jesus Christ our Lord. In other words, eternal life abounds when we are in and under the lordship of Jesus Christ. That means anyone who isn't in Him as Lord is experiencing death and lifelessness. It is sin and death having rule.

Why would a lack of lordship be anything like sin? The definition for sin is simply missing the mark that God has established. Let's look again at the parable of the sower (Matt. 13). Not all seeds live and produce a harvest. Those missing-the-mark seeds produce death. Nothing living comes from them. The mark of pure, healthy, receptive, surrendered-to-the-Lord-Jesus heart-soil was literally missed in those other cases.

The names we continually empower, the thoughtless phrases that fall from our mouths that magnify and release all kinds of other powers, those are the lords who will happily supply the food we have become addicted to. That kind of food isn't the Word of God or the Word of Life. If Jesus is Lord, His Word is Lord, and His Word will be the bread of life for your daily sustenance.

The opposite of the Word of God as eternal truth is the word of the father of lies as eternal death. Because he is the counterfeiter, he will bring to life every scripture for his benefit as long as he is released as lord in your now. He will capitalize on your ignorance and on your innocent and naive following of the world's influence around you.

Perhaps any attempt we make in our own strength and ability to live out any of these areas could become empty and legalistic. But to really know the GREAT I AM, to be fully immersed and saturated in Him daily, results in an authentic, non-legalistic, grace-soaked surrender to His lordship with an accompanying abundant-life kind of evidence.

The God of all grace has given us and continues to give us His grace, mercy, and favor as we endeavor to live yielded, forgiven lives as releasers of salvation. To assume there is no active pursuit on our part would be to allow self and sin to trample on the cross of Christ while we force the abundance of grace to cover our willful disobedience to the work of the Lord.

God's Word is full of conditional words and phrases such as *if, remain, seek, ask, knock, cry out, call upon, keep being filled,* and so on. Let's look at a few of them.

> *If you remain in me and my words remain in you, ask whatever you wish, and it will be done for you. This is to my Father's glory, that you bear much fruit, showing yourselves to be my disciples.*
>
> —John 15:7–8

> *I tell you, even though he will not get up and give you the bread because of friendship, yet because of your shameless audacity he will surely get up and give you as much as you need.*
>
> —Luke 11:8

He knows us, and He knows our hearts are easily turned and persuaded. His insistence on our constant pursuit of Him and His lordship isn't egomaniacally driven. He calls us to such a life of pressing in and pursuit of Him because it is in our best interest and because it will result in the best release of His kingdom.

The Lord wants to be in us in everything that He needs from us in order to accomplish His will on earth. That is the true definition of an intimate, ongoing relationship that is fully expressed and made manifest under His lordship. Every void and crack in this relationship will be exploited by the enemy in an attempt to destroy the ongoing work of salvation that should be flowing out of us.

The strategy of our enemy is to take advantage of the powerful truth of Romans 10:9–10, 13 for his purposes to fill our lives with the anti-kingdom of God. He knows the words we say will empower lords. He knows we will say the words that come from the contents of our hearts. He knows that the contents of our hearts come from what we are continually exposed to.

And those things come at a price, part of the cycle of releasing salvation, part of the transfer out of and into results in a sacrificial walking away and letting go of this life as we know it.

No one who has left home or brothers or sisters or mother or father or children or fields for me and the gospel will fail to receive a hundred times as much in this present age . . . and in the age to come eternal life.
—Mark 10:29–30

What is it that Jesus insists we leave? Is He literally asking us to denounce our earthly families and move to an undisclosed location in Montana so we may inherit the fullness of the kingdom? That wouldn't be my interpretation. He is laying down the litmus test that challenges our heart loyalty. This charge leaves no other lords as an option.

Jesus Christ Lord I am is requiring total heart surrender and total lordship to be first priority in our lives. He shows us the condition of the heart that claims to be loyal but in the end cannot surrender the remaining kingdom territory to Him. "If you want to be perfect, go, sell your possessions . . . and you will have treasure in heaven" (Matt. 19:21).

His name is His nature, and His nature is both what we need from Him and what He needs from us. When we submit and surrender to His lordship, when we confess with our mouth continually, we will remain in His perfect will.

We are asked to forsake all else for Him and for the gospel of the kingdom. The good news is that heaven's kingdom is possible now and so much better than the life we so desperately cling to. Jesus is Lord of the kingdom. And every name He is known by must be honored and declared as Lord.

It is our decision. We can cling to family and land to the degree that they take priority over the lordship of Jesus, and we will receive the fruit of that decision. We will have earthly and temporary rule in the matters of this life.

Or we can forsake all and submit to His lordship, surrendering our family and land and affairs to His lordship and, as a result, suffer some persecution for doing so.

The choice results in His desired fullness in this life, in this present age, as well as seeing His kingdom expand and His miracles flow, His fullness is released, and His total deliverance starts now and continues into eternity.

CHAPTER SIX

Wisdom: The Lord of Wisdom

First come, first served. The priorities we put first get our first focus, our first attention. It isn't just that those who come first will be served first; it is that we will end up serving those we have given first place to.

When we seek first the kingdom of God, we are being obedient to God's order. He is pleading for us throughout scripture to seek first His will and His way. He knows best for us that what is first sets the order of the rest.

Just think about it this way. First, seek. The first thing to do is to seek. Not think. Not act. Not do. The very phrase is a call to allow wisdom to occupy the first place in divine order.

Why is there a chapter on wisdom in a book about the matters of lordship? Because I believe that at the root of every misapplication of God's Word is the failure to keep Jesus LORD I AM WISDOM as first place. When He as wisdom is first, all doctrine, all action, all Christ-centered living will be rightly aligned with the counsel of His will.

"I was appointed in ages past at the very first, before the earth began" (Prov. 8:23 NLT). It is clear from this passage that wisdom was at the very beginning. Wisdom was a first among firsts. Many teachers and scholars use the book of Hebrews to focus on the role of faith as the primary force of creation. By faith the worlds were framed. That is true. "By faith we understand that the universe was formed" (Heb. 11:3).

But while God spoke the world into existence by faith, it was through wisdom that the universe was planned. Remember, wisdom was present before faith was released. I believe that before faith speaks, it is wisdom that dictates what should be spoken by faith.

"In the beginning the Word already existed.... The Word gave life to everything that was created" (John 1:1, 4 NLT). The Word of God was the beginning, and wisdom was there at the beginning. Jesus as the Word Lord I am Wisdom was the transmitter for creation. Creation came through Him. It was Jesus as the Word who gave life.

Wisdom was the first specific expression of a name of the Lord. Before salvation, before provision, before captain of the host, before any other name of the Lord we are given in scripture, Wisdom was the first. Look again at this.

I was appointed in ages past, at the very first, before the earth began.
—Prov. 8:23 NLT

Wisdom is the principal thing,
—Prov. 4:7 NKJV

The law of first mention can then bring context to how we interpret the importance of wisdom throughout scripture. The law of first mention is an interpretive guide that states that when a biblical theme is mentioned first in scripture, it is normative to expect that mention to have established context for the ensuing instances where that same theme appears. Wisdom as Jesus was literally first, before Jesus as faith, before the creation of light or the universe. Even though wisdom isn't directly mentioned first in the book of Genesis in the creation account, because Jesus as wisdom was there, wisdom was there.

Wisdom first as Lord I am Wisdom gave birth to and subsequently released every other manifold expression of the Word of God into reality. And in doing so, it set in motion every principle that would hold together the universe and establish His kingdom forever.

His name is Jesus, and His name is Wisdom. As far as ancient manuscripts go, the book of Job was authored before Genesis. The Holy Spirit revealed this truth as the written Word of God. Jesus Christ Lord I am Wisdom is the one being spoken of. "The fear of the Lord is true wisdom; to forsake evil is real understanding" (Job 28:28 NLT).

Wisdom: The Lord of Wisdom

Wisdom is the fear of whom? The LORD I AM. The fear of the Lord is true wisdom. Let me write that in a different way. To know Jesus Christ LORD I AM is to know Him as Wisdom. To have the ultimate reverential fear and revelation of Him as Lord begins with knowing Him as Wisdom.

We humans have nothing to offer as far as wisdom and knowledge. But under His lordship as the only wise God, we can watch Him release His incredible kingdom through us as willing participants. With the lens of wisdom as Lord established as priority, other key truths from scripture begin to take on an even more powerful understanding regarding matters of lordship.

The power of God and the wisdom of God are inseparable. If we want to release His power, we must surrender to Jesus as LORD I AM WISDOM, and we must speak in line with that understanding.

> *But to those called by God to salvation, both Jews and Gentiles, Christ is the power of God and the wisdom of God.*
> —1 Cor. 1:24 NLT

Jesus Christ as Lord of salvation is both power and wisdom—not one without the other, but both. No power, no salvation. No wisdom, no salvation. They are incomplete without the other. I alluded earlier in this book to the truth of salvation equating to true wholeness. Salvation, then, is being made whole to a reality.

So Jesus is LORD I AM WISDOM, and through Him, the power of God unto salvation (wholeness to His reality) is then released. Take a look at some references in succession that enforce this truth.

> *God has united you with Christ Jesus. For our benefit God made him to be wisdom itself.*
> —1 Cor. 1:30 NLT

> *All glory to the only wise God, through Jesus Christ, forever. Amen.*
> —Rom. 16:27 NLT

> *Now unto the King eternal, immortal, invisible, the only wise God, be honour and glory for ever and ever. Amen.*
> —1 Timothy 1:17 KJV

To the only wise God our Saviour, be glory and majesty, dominion and power, both now and ever. Amen.

—Jude 1:25 KJV

The truth is underscored when we look at these passages together. The Word was in the beginning. Wisdom is priority. His name is His nature. Jesus Christ Lord I am Wisdom is the primary catalyst in releasing salvation. Wisdom is vital to wholeness according to the divine order of God. In fact, wisdom is the divine order part that is needed. Wisdom as the order of God through Jesus Christ Lord I am is essential and must supersede our carnal understanding.

Think about your life for a moment. We often wait longer than we think we need to when we are waiting for God to move. Yet during that waiting time, He isn't torturing us unnecessarily. No, He is wisely ordering all things rightly according to His kingdom under the Lordship of Jesus Christ.

We look back on our path, and in hindsight, we sometimes see how beautifully orchestrated and well-ordered everything was. What was taking place during that time? Jesus Lord I am Wisdom was having His way. How much more strategic and effective do you think we could be if we let wisdom as Lord I am be our first line of seeking, the first name we call upon in every situation?

The Apostle Paul frequently expressed Jesus Lord as Wisdom. Paul rightly had the full revelation from the Holy Spirit of the importance of the lordship of Jesus as wisdom first. "That the God of our Lord Jesus Christ, the Father of glory, may give unto you the spirit of wisdom and revelation in the knowledge of him" (Eph. 1:17 KJV).

What is the prayer here? That we are filled with the spirit of love? Faith? Miracles? Doctrine? No, his passionate prayer for the body of Christ, the church on earth, opened with wisdom. The knowledge of—or we could say the intimate knowing of—the person of Jesus as expressed in the spirit of wisdom and revelation is what Paul is praying for.

When Jesus as Wisdom is Lord, when He as Wisdom is sought first, the fullness of every other aspect of His name, His nature, His Word, His purpose, His will, and much more can be released precisely, redemptively, and powerfully on earth today.

How would our lives be different if we made a daily discipline of seeking the Lord and asking Him for wisdom before we did anything else? It seems to me there is good biblical support that encourages us to do just that.

Without a revelation in the heart, there is no authentic confession of lordship, and there can be no genuine salvation experience. I can't say definitely that God isn't going to save in a situation where our own weaknesses may be keeping us from a healthy heart-revelation. I would say that the daily doses of wholeness God desires to release in our lives won't be as abundant or evident as they could be.

In other words, there will be much less of a releasing of wholeness to His reality. His will is made known, and our purpose is ordered and released because Jesus is Lord I am Wisdom.

Wherein he hath abounded toward us in all wisdom and prudence; Having made known unto us the mystery of his will, according to his good pleasure which he hath purposed in himself.

—Eph. 1:8–9 KJV

Wisdom makes known. Wisdom reveals every other thing. Jesus as Wisdom is the key. His will is made known to us through the spirit of wisdom and revelation to release salvation. Not just so we would repent of our sins and ask to receive salvation at some point in the past, but so we tap into Him as Wisdom and call upon Him continually to release salvation in His name.

What could happen if the Lord of wisdom was in firm authority in our lives and our ongoing confession was releasing a saving kingdom of wisdom and revelation? Jesus has poured Himself out, abundantly expressed as wisdom so we can know the fullness of His nature and walk in His perfect will. It actually brings pleasure to the Lord when we seek Him, worship Him, and declare Him as wisdom. "We ask God to give you complete knowledge of his will and to give you spiritual wisdom and understanding" (Col. 1:9 NLT).

Paul continually pleads to know Him as wisdom. So here it is again. The "complete knowledge of his will" comes from spiritual wisdom and understanding. It is at the top of the list of the things the Apostle Paul is praying and declaring over the church.

The result of this prayer for wisdom and this seeking of wisdom is a fruitful life in the kingdom of God, fulfilling the perfect will of God. It is also an essential part of spiritual growth and discipleship in the Lord.

God's Word establishes that Jesus is Wisdom and that wisdom is at the beginning of everything. So it stands to reason that in our seeking first kingdom matters, wisdom is a first of firsts. Without wisdom, we are lost and don't know how to pray, to walk, to minister, to plan, or to live the abundant kingdom life we are called to live in an effective manner. "But seek first his kingdom and his righteousness, and all these things will be given to you as well" (Matt. 6:33).

The kingdom of the Lord must be confessed and believed in order for life in the kingdom to be aligned rightly. Righteousness is doing and being right according to seeking first. Everything else comes as a result. Without wisdom and without the Lord of wisdom revealing and releasing His truth, everything else is highly prone to error. Apart from the spirit of wisdom, religion is the worst version of itself. Cultic practices and false doctrines are birthed, and all kinds of evil work abound.

Where self-seeking ambition exists, so does strife. James calls it disorder and every evil practice. Does that sound like your local church? Is it full of disorder and strife? Does that kind of description fit your family gatherings and inhabit your friendship circles? When that is the case, it is clearly the absence of any kind of surrender to the lordship of Jesus allowing the spirit of wisdom and revelation to lead peaceably and fruitfully. The antidote or, more accurately, the preventative measure is found in Jesus as Wisdom released through salvation, bringing the wholeness of His kingdom to the earth now.

> *But if you harbor bitter envy and selfish ambition in your hearts, do not boast about it or deny the truth. Such "wisdom" does not come down from heaven but is earthly, unspiritual, demonic. For where you have envy and selfish ambition, there you find disorder and every evil practice. But the wisdom that comes from heaven is first of all pure; then peace-loving, considerate, submissive, full of mercy and good fruit, impartial and sincere.*
>
> —James 3:14–17

Wisdom: The Lord of Wisdom

When the Word of God, inspired by the Holy Spirit, talks to us about wisdom, the living Word is talking to us about Jesus as wisdom. Some people get confused when wisdom is referred to as a woman. In the Hebrew language, the word for *wisdom* is a feminine noun, so it was natural for Solomon (and the writers of Hebrew poetry) to personify wisdom as a woman. That doesn't mean wisdom is a separate female spirit of some kind. To assume that would be a misinterpretation of those passages and to misapply the truth found in these poetic writings.

However, wisdom does call to us, and we are to cry out for wisdom. We are to specifically call upon the name of the Lord as wisdom and allow an intimate relationship with Him as wisdom to be expressed in us, to us, and through us in every aspect of our lives. "The beginning of wisdom is this: Get wisdom. Though it cost all you have, get understanding" (Prov. 4:7).

Every word of God is a wise word. His commands, His precepts, His truths all are released and revealed through Jesus Christ as Lord. Jesus as Wisdom rightly divides and shows us the correct application of His truth. The result of that is understanding. In ancient Hebrew culture, understanding meant living obediently to the truth.

That doesn't take place with a nod of agreement; it happens when it is a painful sacrifice to live in a way that goes against the grain of society. We can't use our current culture as a measure and still rightly interpret the Word of truth. That would be backward. Wisdom measures truth against the Word of God and nothing else. Jesus as Wisdom is unrelenting in His call for us to surrender and confess Him as Lord.

Wisdom shouts in the streets.
She cries out in the public square . . .
"How long, you simpletons,
will you insist on being simpleminded? . . .
I'll share my heart with you and make you wise."

—Prov. 1:20, 22–23 NLT

He desires to make us wise. He desires that we rule as He does, as lords over this world, in full dominion under His lordship and authority, expanding His kingdom and releasing His power.

God clearly separates the human fleshly kind of wisdom from spiritual wisdom. To get a clear picture of that, we have to see Jesus as Lord of Wisdom in our lives in a way that pulls the spiritual eternal truth (transcending time) into our present and into our now, or *chronos* (measured, quantitative time). As a result, we can ensure that His *kairos* (opportune moment, perfect timing) causes His kingdom and His redemptive purpose to be fully expressed and released.

That is a powerful revelation of the potential of Jesus Lord of Wisdom being declared and surrendered to consistently and actively. A sinner's prayer spoken once or a stirring chorus of "He Is Lord" isn't going to get that done.

> *We do, however, speak a message of wisdom among the mature, but not the wisdom of this age or of the rulers of this age, who are coming to nothing. No, we declare God's wisdom.*
> —1 Cor. 2:6–7

We could also say that we declare Jesus the true spiritual wisdom exalted over all. The wisdom of this age and the rulers of this age are coming to nothing. So if the wisdom of this age is what you exalt—in other words, what you make lord—you have the fruit of the kingdom of the lord of the wisdom of this age. God's Word says it will amount to nothing.

So you have a nice house, a great job, and an amazing 401(k). It will amount to nothing. All the things we've leveraged—our current economic system, the political landscape, consumer-driven appetites—any of it apart from the wisdom of God will be a worthless investment. His kingdom and the commodities He uses to expand it should confound us and not make perfect sense in the world system. Let the god of this world navigate the ways of this world.

If, on the other hand, you exalt the name of the Lord as Wisdom, if you worship and magnify the wisdom that is from above, you will walk in the kingdom of that wisdom. You will experience the fruit of that kingdom.

> *But the wisdom that comes from heaven is first of all pure; then peace-loving, considerate, submissive, full of mercy and good fruit, impartial and sincere.*
> —James 3:17

Why is this wisdom from heaven? Because Jesus as the Word is forever settled in heaven, and He is wisdom.

Wisdom: The Lord of Wisdom

Your word, LORD, is eternal; it stands firm in the heavens.
—Ps. 119:89

Heaven and earth will pass away, but my words will never pass away.
—Luke 21:33

The passage in James shows us that wisdom is fruit-bearing and, in fact, full of fruit. Jesus is Lord of the harvest. He is all about increasing fruit and releasing fruit that remains.

This is what we speak, not in words taught us by human wisdom but in words taught by the Spirit, explaining spiritual realities with Spirit-taught words.
—1 Cor. 2:13

It is vital that the Lord Jesus as Wisdom be released in the Spirit of Wisdom in a way that opens up the power and application of God's Word to us, in us, and through us. While the world marches on in darkness and lack of understanding, the person submitted to the lordship of Jesus in His person and expression as wisdom will walk in discernment and application of spiritual matters. That anchors the body of Christ in Holy-Spirit-breathed truth and inoculates against secular, seductively clothed, spiritual-sounding, Christian-like doctrine.

Antinomianism is a doctrine that promotes liberty to sin willfully because of the grace of God offered in salvation. Legalism is the opposite extreme that doesn't reflect the whole counsel of the Word of God and promotes sanctification through adherence to the Law. The demonstration of something supernatural or miraculous does not always point to the presence of the Lord Jesus as the source (2 Thess. 2:9, Matt. 24:24).

The mind of Christ is a renewed mind in the Word of God. The mind of Christ remains in us only as long as we remain in Christ. The carnal mind isn't the mind of Christ. The carnal mind is against God. The carnal mind stays unrenewed and unsubmitted to the lordship of Jesus as Wisdom.

Do not conform to the pattern of this world, but be transformed by the renewing of your mind. Then you will be able to test and approve what God's will is—his good, pleasing and perfect will.
—Rom. 12:2

Lordship Matters

The mind governed by the flesh is death, but the mind governed by the Spirit is life and peace. The mind governed by the flesh is hostile to God; it does not submit to God's law, nor can it do so. Those who are in the realm of the flesh cannot please God.
—Rom. 8:6–8

I like that the word *governed* is used here because it brings us back to rule and lordship. Submission to God's law is submission to Jesus as Word forever settled in heaven. Submission to God's law as revealed by the Spirit of Wisdom and revelation in the knowledge of Him results in true life and true peace as it exists in the kingdom of heaven.

We release the kingdom of heaven onto earth when we declare and submit to the government of Jesus as Wisdom, the only wise God.

His intent was that now, through the church, the manifold wisdom of God should be made known to the rulers and authorities in the heavenly realms, according to his eternal purpose that he accomplished in Christ Jesus our Lord.
—Eph. 3:10–11

If our minds were daily renewed and surrendered to the lordship of Jesus in every aspect of His nature, wouldn't the territory of the King be firmly established? Wouldn't the King and Lord who is declared in power and authority have an army of kingdom inhabitants all living and moving and having their being in the lordship of Jesus Christ?

What does a body of believers look like who walk so naturally under the lordship and reign of Jesus that signs and wonders follow? What does it look like when Jesus as Wisdom is exalted and our lives are so flowing in discernment and precision in every prayer, every matter, and every human interaction we encounter?

You are still worldly. For since there is jealousy and quarreling among you, are you not worldly? Are you not acting like mere humans? For when one says, "I follow Paul," and another, "I follow Apollos," are you not mere human beings?
—1 Cor. 3:3–4

It's interesting that the sub-heavenly minded and non-kingdom-like behavior of those carnal Christians stemmed from divided loyalties among earthly leaders. Jesus wasn't truly remaining as Lord to those Corinthians. Paul had become lord, and Apollos had become lord. And because they allowed strife to occupy their attention and affection, ultimately Satan, the father of lies, was operating as their lord.

It is vital to get a full understanding of who Jesus as Lord really is. Knowing and releasing Him into our now as wisdom is the beginning.

CHAPTER SEVEN

Finally

Have you fully repented of everything that denies the revelation of the truth that Jesus Christ is Lord? Are you, with the entirety of your being, bowing low and confessing with your whole life's existence that Jesus Christ is Lord?

Maybe for the first time, the Lord is making that a reality for you. I want to invite you to literally get down on your knees wherever you are and cry out to the Lord with all your heart. Declare that you need Him more than anything or anyone. And in whatever way that pours out of your heart, give Him the place He deserves as Lord.

In doing so, you will be calling on the name of the Lord Jesus. And you will be confessing with your mouth the revelation of your heart. A new nature will be released to you and ratified into your now reality. You are saved, delivered, healed, whole, and made new in every way possible.

But don't stop there. Repent daily from anything that doesn't belong to Jesus, and give yourself entirely to obediently serve Him, listen to Him, and follow Him in every way.

If you aren't faithfully and consistently attending a local Christian church, start immediately. The local church is the pathway for you to learn and continue to grow alongside others who are living as a testimony to Jesus Christ to the glory of God the Father.

Study the Word of God in as many translations as possible, and apply your heart to understanding by giving ear to solid, grounded, word of truth Bible teachers and leaders.

Pour out your heart constantly to the Lord in prayer and devotion to Him. There is no perfect way. He will respond to you as you sincerely seek Him with all your heart.

You are now born again and saved to an ever-renewing, ongoing flow of the kingdom of God that is pouring through you, empowered by the Holy Spirit, making you whole and bringing wholeness to others under the Lordship of Jesus Christ to the glory of God the Father.

The Hinge of God's Love

We all live on the razor's edge of the Law of Lordship. That means that in so many ways, it is simple for us to undermine the truth of God's Word and hinder the Lord I am from establishing and expanding the kingdom of God through us.

Daily, we are challenged with the temptation to make our faith a religion that binds us to methods, forms, and orders and replaces our existence as being known only by the Lord I am. We tend to picture the Pharisee as anyone but us. Yet we all can be guilty of elevating human rules in our lives and missing the heart of God's love in the process (Matt. 15:8). The answer isn't leaving the church or abandoning our faith; it is keeping in mind the reason for our faith.

> *Jesus replied: "'Love the Lord your God with all your heart and with all your soul and with all your mind.' This is the first and greatest commandment. And the second is like it: 'Love your neighbor as yourself.' All the Law and the Prophets hang on these two commandments."*
>
> —Matt. 22:37–40

This truth pivots on the hinge of divine love. Jesus Christ is Lord I am Love. God is love, and He is pure love. When love is the key, kingdom salvation in Christ Jesus is released. When love is absent, the kingdom of darkness is released. And the result is an entirely different version of my expanded paraphrase of Romans 10:9–10, 13. Let's think back to the early pages of this book where I first paraphrased this passage in a positive way, establishing the lordship of Jesus and the releasing of His kind of salvation. Without a revelation of divine love, the following idea is the result.

> The sum total of all of your utterances and actions as you live for self results in a continual releasing of the complete and perfect wholeness contained in the false truths of the enemy, establishing and expanding the kingdom of darkness on earth while manifesting the perfect will of the god of this world as lord.

There is a constant battle that either confirms the revelation that Jesus Christ is Lord I am or it dilutes, detracts, and destroys that revelation from being a now released reality as salvation in Christ Jesus. When self speaks, the enemy wins, and he is enforced as lord.

Here is why this charge from the Apostle Paul is so vital for us to receive and apply daily to our lives.

So then, my dear ones, just as you have always obeyed [my instructions with enthusiasm], not only in my presence, but now much more in my absence, continue to work out your salvation [that is, cultivate it, bring it to full effect, actively pursue spiritual maturity] with awe-inspired fear and trembling [using serious caution and critical self-evaluation to avoid anything that might offend God or discredit the name of Christ].

—Phil. 2:12 AMP

A Blessing Prayer and a Picture of Salvation

May he give you what your heart desires and fulfill your whole purpose.
—Ps. 20:4 CSB

There are many similar verses, but I particularly love this passage. I regularly pray it over myself, my family, my coworkers, and my neighborhood. Our built-in need is for the Lord, so when we ask Him to give us our heart's desire, we are asking for more of Him. We cry out, "Lord, place within me the desires that align with Your name and Your nature so the fulfillment of Your will, to release salvation into this fallen world in me and around me, becomes the fulfillment of my purpose. To fulfill Your purpose, Lord, is the perfect fulfillment of my purpose."

Consistent Lordship Confessions

In order to help my daily posture remain under the lordship of Jesus Christ, I have found it helpful to declare and decree very specifically the names and natures that He lovingly desires for me to experience.

Here is a model and guide for that. You can fill in the name and nature of the Lord that is most needed for the day or that is placed upon your heart as you inquire of Him. The key name and nature in this prayer is in parentheses so you can substitute other names and natures.

Use the prayer as a model and guide, but be free to express from your heart the same ideas in your own words in the language you use to pray and petition the Lord.

Prayer

Lord Jesus, You are my (peace). I am in desperate need of You and only You to lead, guide, protect, and direct me in all of Your (peaceful) paths and ways. I praise You and thank You, Lord, for providing an inexhaustible supply of Your (peace) for me to access and walk in every second of every minute of every hour of every day.

I turn from any other pursuit and any other substitute, and I refuse to call on any other name in any way and at any time than the name of the Lord Jesus Christ. Where my faith falls short, help my unbelief.

Where I am fueling wrong beliefs, open the eyes of my understanding so I can turn away from them, turn back to You, and be filled only with the revelation of Your truth—the Word of truth, Jesus Christ my Lord.

When my words pour from a corrupt or tainted heart, from a place of woundedness, bitterness, legalism, humanistic wisdom, or other earthly identity, help me to repent, refrain, and resist those temptations.

Most of all today, Lord, be in me who You need me to be in order to release wholeness, salvation, and the perfect will of heaven onto earth today. Keep me mindful at every moment that I have declared and will continue to declare with my mouth and with my life's testimony that You, Jesus Christ, LORD I AM, are the Lord of my life and Lord of all the earth. Amen.

Declarations

Just like the model prayer, this declaration can be expressed in your own words and with the specific name and nature of the Lord that is the greatest point of your need as you pray.

I have the (peace) of the Lord in my life because the Lord of (peace) is the Lord of my life. I carry and release His (peace) everywhere I go. I am an able minister to the world in need of the Lord of (peace). My identity is secure in Him as I rest in the (peace) that only the Lord of (Peace) has to offer.

I am with the Lord of (peace) in and through every storm. The people around me are ministered to by the great level of (peace) that I carry under the lordship of the Lord of (Peace), Jesus Christ. Because of the (peace) I hold, many are drawn into a lasting Lord-declaring, Lord-needing, Lord-saving relationship. And they will be translated out of the kingdom of darkness and into the kingdom of His lasting peace. Because I walk with and live under the shadow of the Mighty Lord Jesus I am, I have (peace) every day.

The Word of God Fueling Belief

As you become disciplined to think differently and speak differently, your life will drastically change. I encourage you to begin to see Christ as Lord in every book, every chapter, and every verse of the Bible. Search and discover how the rich passages of scripture can be a point of expanding and growing your faith and your prayer life as you see the Laws of Lordship come to bear on your life.

There are many great benedictions in the Apostle Paul's epistles, but I want to leave you with the one below as a prayer of encouragement and exhortation. What if we lived according to this scripture passage? What if we constantly surrendered our lives to the name and nature of the Lord Jesus Christ? What if He was allowed to dwell in us so richly that we walked consistently in wisdom? It might be then that our lives would sing a melody to the Lord. It might be then that our grateful existence would be lived out loud as a living testimony empowered by the name of the Lord Jesus Christ.

Let the word of Christ dwell in you richly in all wisdom, teaching and admonishing one another in psalms and hymns and spiritual songs, singing with grace in your hearts to the Lord. And whatever you do in word or deed, do all in the name of the Lord Jesus, giving thanks to God the Father through Him.

—Col. 3:16–17 NKJV

Acknowledgments

My wife, Christine, deserves unending praise for her love and encouragement that so often fuel my empty creative tank so that God's purpose will continue to flourish in the life we share together. She is the true definition of life support, and she is a shining example of a woman who sacrificially serves the Lord with joy and beauty.

For butterfly kisses, clever movie quotes, and winning the hardest hugger contest every time—Allegra. You shine as a reminder of my lively hope in the love of the Lord Jesus Christ. You believe I am Superman, and because of that, so do I.

Thank you, Natalie Hanemann, the perfect editor for me. You were indispensable in bringing this manuscript to the best place of receptivity for the audience the Lord has on His heart. My writing is forever better because of you.

Thank you, Charlana Kelly, for being a lifelong friend to Christine and me and for being positioned as a dream instigator in my life. You lead by example and bless so many. Surely, this book lives in large part because of you.

Pastor Tim Gilligan, thank you for your down-to-earth and incredibly clear teaching style that so resonates with me to this day. Your lasting influence is a vital component of the way I think, process, teach, and write.

Pastor Walt Healy, you are a mentor to mentors. The expression of who I am is marked by your influence and the profound insight into scripture you possess. Certainly, you have indirectly written a large portion of this book because of your teachings that still resonate in my life.

I am so grateful for the incredibly gifted Kristen Barker. Her amazing creative eye for photography made the headshot for this book absolutely perfect.

I give tremendous thanks to the entire team at Lucid Books. They saw the potential in this manuscript. They not only gave it a shot but put a team of experts together to give it life. Each and every one of you is amazing!

"There is no more important issue or subject than lordship. And as the title of James Wheeler's book declares, lordship matters. Having known and worked with James for years, I am not surprised at his thorough, in-depth, and creative approach to this vital topic. I believe that when heart and head work together, we end up with something sacred and relevant. James presents his honest journey of discovering more of the depths and joys of the endless truths and power of the lordship of Jesus. I commend to you James and his timely book. May the title and text continue to inform and remind us that lordship matters."

—**Pastor Tim Gilligan**, DMin,
Founding and Senior Pastor, Meadowbrook Church, Ocala, Florida

"James Wheeler, a man of great character, is probably the most introspective man I know, which makes *Lordship Matters*, a must-read if you want to give yourself more fully to God. James offers a fresh, meditative way to discern and pursue the process of moving into a place of unconditional surrender. He challenges the reader to think and speak differently, and he offers a practical means to achieve success. James lives this way and is therefore qualified to explain it in his own unique way. I highly recommend this book for every serious Christian desiring to seek God with all their heart. God has said that when you do, He will meet you in that place!"

—**Walt Healy**,
Pastor, Author of *Living the Apostles' Creed*,
Founder, The Church of Grace and Peace, Toms River, New Jersey

"James Wheeler has unearthed wisdom for the ages through revelatory insight about the matters of lordship and has captured the essence and power of living a life completely surrendered to Jesus Lord I am. Today, many believers are caught between a cultural Christianity and the reality of Jesus's ultimate purpose for their lives. As a result, they are missing a vital key and the blessing that accompanies it. In *Lordship Matters*, James masterfully guides the reader with life experience and practical application to the place God prepared for us long ago. This book is simply a must-read for every person who calls themselves a believer."

—**Charlana Kelly**,
Pastor, Author, Speaker, Entrepreneur, and Lover of Jesus